Praise for Unbroke

MW01289525

"Jeremy has given us a raw and open look at his life and family, both good and bad. His honesty allows all of us to vicariously assess the strength of our own commitment to our families and to see possible warning signs ahead. It also gives us a great portrait of Gods grace in real life, and the hope that He truly can redeem even our biggest failures."

- Brett Rickey, Pastor of Highland Park Church, Author of Boomerang and Chasing Cool

"Jeremy's story is neither boring nor sensational—and it's not wrapped up with a 'happily ever after' ending. His story is as real as it is relatable, and he shares it without pretense alongside the wisdom he's gained along the way. Any leader will benefit from Unbroken, but especially those who live under the spotlight of ministry."

- Tim Stevens, Author of Vision: Lost & Found and Pop Goes the Church

"Unbroken is an apt word to describe the man or woman who trusts and perseveres in the Lord through difficult times. The narrative in the pages of Unbroken is a story of brokenness when things fall apart, and yet healing as the Lord begins to put lives back together again. Jeremy gives us a glimpse of that process from its roots to a place of restoration. Knowing that we all have moments of great need for restoration, the reader will find an engaging and hopeful story that teaches us to reach from the pit to the pinnacle."

- Dr. Mark Gregory, Pastor, Calvary Baptist Church, Author of Net Trigger and The Crossing Ward

"Honesty. Humility. Hope. These three words capture the real heart behind Jeremy Johnson's Unbroken. For anyone who's life has ever taken an unexpected u-turn--leaving you hopeless, confused, and heartbroken--Jeremy's journey will inspire and encourage you to refocus and get back in the game. Unbroken will help you understand that defeat can be life-changing in the most positive of ways, if you only allow it."

– **Adam York**, Editor, Collegiate Magazine

"I didn't know how much I needed Unbroken, for me, until I finished. It reminded me that my story is the most powerful thing I can share with others. Unbroken will remind you why the journey is important and necessary. Your best days are in front of you! Keep pressing and don't give up on your dreams. I am so excited for the book tour to come to Life Church so people can take the steps to move from broken to Unbroken!"

- **Chris Hughes**, Lead Pastor, Life Church-Franklin, NC

"Jeremy Johnson is living proof that God is not nearly as concerned about what happens to us as He is to how we respond to what happens. It is what happens to us that molds and shapes more to the image of Christ if we submit to the process. Jeremy has submitted to the process and what could have driven him away from God has driven him to the Father. He has chosen to not simply "go" through the storm but to" grow" through the storm."

-**Ron Cook,** Founder and President. Care for Pastors

"Jeremy Johnson states in the introduction of his new book unbroken, "the reason I wrote this book was to share my story with transparency." Jeremy does exactly that. Unbroken is an honest encouraging look at the work of God in the life of a man yielded to Him. I was blessed by Jeremy and by reading this book"

-Travis Jones- Teaching Pastor, Silverdale Baptist Church

"Unbroken" is the unfiltered and authentic journey of a man of God who tastes the pain and failures of life but experiences the restoration of God. Jeremy's transparent journey births hope in the hearts of the hopeless and even stands as a helpful warning to those who have priorities out of order. You may fall but you can start over. As one who experienced the process of restoration first hand, Jeremy reveals that although the vessel may be marred and messed up, it is still in the hand of the Potter. This is the message of God's love and this is the beautiful testimony of my friend Jeremy Johnson."

-Kevin Wallace- Lead Pastor, Redemption Point Church

"As a church planting coach, I have worked with dozens of planters over the years. I have seen many things that can crush a planter and his family. Jeremy shares, in a transparent way, what is far too often hidden in planters. Jeremy gives warnings and hope for all who need to deal with what may really be going on behind the scenes for a planter.Every church planter should take the short time needed to read this real, crushing and unfortunately, very common account of a planter."

-Gary Baldus, Founding Pastor of New Walk Church & Church Planting Coach

Unbroken

Discovering Wholeness Through the Shattered Pieces of Life

JEREMY JOHNSON

DEDICATION

Dedicated to the memory of my father,
Stewart Johnson.
The ultimate example of the Unbroken!

CONTENTS

Chapter 8- **Change Can Happen**

RT- *The moment we realize that we are not the hero of our own story and that Jesus is, is the moment we allow God's power to be activated in us.*

Chapter 9- **Pain is Never Wasted**

RT- *He can turn the ugliest piece of dirt, a part that has been lost in the ashes and transform them into the most beautiful creature known to man.*

Chapter 10- **The Process**

RT- *Sometimes we have to go through the mud, spit and dirtiness of life to get to the good stuff.*

Chapter 11- **52 Day Journey**

RT- *Even when the walls are shaking, keep singing, your breakthrough is coming!*

Chapter 12- **Divine Interruptions**

RT- *God doesn't ask us to see the whole puzzle until the end of our lives. He wants us to simply lay down one piece at a time and allow Him to shape the rest of the big picture.*

Chapter 13- **The Comeback**

RT- *Things may look simply impossible, just remember, that is the moment God stages His greatest comebacks.*

#unbrokenthebook

INTRODUCTION

Un-bro-ken- To be whole or intact.

All of my life I have heard the nursery rhyme about Humpty Dumpty, a simple four line riddle about an egg that sits on a wall and then falls from his lofty perch. Of course it is never a good thing when an egg falls from anywhere because brokenness is inevitable. The rhyme describes a scene of "all the kings horses and all the kings men" attempting to put this poor fellow back together, but failing miserably. We never hear another verse about what happens to Humpty Dumpty, his fate seemingly sealed by his brokenness.

That's the end of the story, no hope, no positive outcome, just brokenness, the end. It's a sad ending that leaves us all wondering, "that's it?" The reality is we have all experienced our own fall and our own shattered existence. Yes, we have all been Mr. or Ms. Dumpty before. We have all been on that wall where life is good and things are going well only to take a tumble back to a harsh reality. Sometimes, it's our own doing and sometimes there are circumstances that we never see coming that throw us to the ground and leave us lying in shattered pieces.

Much like this story, when we fall brokenness is inevitable. Today our world is filled with broken lives and relationships. We try to medicate the pain with all types of earthly solutions but it never satisfies. There is nothing in this world that can put us back together. We try everything but nothing seems to mend our pieces. The healing power of Jesus is the only thing that transforms us back to wholeness. He is the one that can take what is broken and make it unbroken. Unlike Humpty Dumpty, there is still hope for us. It's not the end of the story.

Many times it is the very thing that jump starts our new chapter.

The definition of the word "whole" is to be complete or full : not lacking or leaving out any part. That is what takes place when we are made unbroken, we are mended by Jesus Christ. He fills the gaps and heals the broken pieces of our lives. He takes an impossible situation, one with a million pieces and restores it back to one piece. He doesn't just restore it back to its natural condition but transforms it into something better than before. Only God can truly restore.

Throughout this book I will unpack the reasons my life became broken, even when I attempted to paint the pretty picture. I will tell you the journey of how God restored me back to Him and how He helped me rediscover my purpose in this world.

Let's face it, the world doesn't need another book that tells us how to do something or what not to do. The reason I wrote this book was to share my story with transparency. I wanted to share my struggles and tell you that if you still have a pulse, there is certain hope for you. Even after the fall from the wall, you can still be pointed in the right direction. I believe that not because I have witnessed it in other people's lives as a spectator, which I have, but because I have lived it. I have been an active participant in the struggle.

I heard Pastor Perry Noble say once, "I am not better than you or smarter than you but I am one of you!" That's certainly true in my case.
I have lived through heartbreak and I have sinned with the best of them, but the good news is, I have grown through the struggle and Christ has strengthened me through the trials. Throughout this book I will share some biblical truths that will

give you hope and bring you out of the depths of your circumstances into the loving arms of Jesus, right where you belong.

This book is for the broken people in the world, which includes all of us. Whether you have been broken by tragedy, divorce, loss, bad relationships or even by disappointment, this book is for you. What unfolds in the following pages is a testimony that God can heal the most broken pieces of your life. The things that have been burned in the chapters of your soul, can be resurrected, just as Jesus Himself was resurrected and conquered the grave. God can take what was broken and make it unbroken.

Through the power of Jesus, you can come back from certain defeat, even when the world tells you it's inconceivable. Through His everlasting grace, restoration will not just be a pipe dream or a lofty ideal, but a vivid reality. Through His love, pure joy can be renewed or maybe even discovered for the first time. Through His mercy, hope will shine through even the darkest corridors of your life. Let the words of this book wash over your soul as encouragement and as a stark reminder that nothing is too difficult for our God to handle and no one is ever too lost to be rescued.

So sit back, relax and let the journey begin.

,D BURN

,ring through the blinds on that Wednesday n. .s time to wake up and roll out of bed. I immeu. checked my phone, as I did every morning, to see what was happening in the world. I quickly scanned through email, Facebook, Twitter and the headlines on the CNN app. I put my phone down and jumped into the shower to continue my normal routine. As I was getting dressed, my wife approached me with a nervous look in her eyes, I knew something was wrong. "I need you to come downstairs", she said. I had no idea what was about to happen, no clue that my whole life would change in the blink of an eye.

I walked down the stairs and to my surprise my mentor was waiting for me. I didn't know what was happening and I was fearful. I sat down on the couch while my wife and mentor stared at me as if they were staring straight through me. My wife began to tear up and she said:

"I'm taking the kids and going to my parents. I still love you and want to be married to you, but you need to get some help and get better."

What was she saying? How could this be happening? My greatest fear had become a heartbreaking reality.

That was the very moment that time stopped in my world and everything changed in my life. That was the very moment that set me on a whirlwind adventure into the unknown. Whether I liked it or not, nothing would ever go back to the way it was.

Spinning Out of Control

I have a fairly decent memory. In fact, I am the self proclaimed king of useless knowledge. For instance, I can tell you the starting lineup for the 1987 Minnesota Twins. The sad thing is, I was only 9 years old in 1987 and I don't even like the Twins. Why would anyone need or want to know that?

While there are many things I choose to remember, there are also certain things in my life that I would rather forget. At the top of that short list is hearing my wife say the words that would change my life forever, words that would absolutely shake my existence.

Nine simple words shattered my heart and woke me up all at the same time. The words, "I'm taking the kids and going to my parents." It was that brief sentence that would flip my world completely upside down and inside out. It was a sentence that would send me on a grueling, painful, wonderfully blessed journey that I never expected. As much as I wish those words were part of a bad dream, they will always be etched in my mind.

Have you ever been told something that literally brings you to your knees? Almost as if someone punched you in the gut? That is certainly what I felt when my wife of 13 years uttered those words to me. I was in complete shock, mostly because I was still in complete denial about my current condition. I thought I had it all together and believed I could fix the things that were wrong with my family and my marriage. I was foolish. Let me paint the picture for you, I was a pastor, a church planter, a husband and a dad of two wonderful children, unfortunately sometimes in that very order.

To say that I had everything that I ever wanted in my life was an understatement. So how did I have this life that I just described, seemingly perfect, and at the same time have a wife that wanted out? On the surface, it didn't make much sense. I tried to tell myself that because once again, nothing was wrong with me. I wasn't the problem, at least in my mind. Everything was great was the lie I was selling to myself and others and I was buying it. The fact of the matter was things weren't going well at all.

My life was spinning out of control so quickly that I was reaching a breaking point. A point I could no longer handle or control. A point that called for drastic, painful measures and it would force me and my wife to make difficult decisions regarding the future. Everything was about to change.

Running on Empty

I am proud of a few things in my life, not so proud of some others. I am unofficially the Guinness World record holder for the guy that has run out of gas more times than anyone in the history of mankind. You can call it laziness, some call it procrastination. I tend to think of it as thrifty. I like to get the last drop out of every tank. (There's a sermon in there somewhere). I haven't done it in a while, but there was a stretch in my early to mid 20s, where I probably ran out of gas more than 10 times. I know it's completely embarrassing to admit.

There have been times, where I would run out and try to restart the car just to make it the last mile before going to the gas station. It worked sometimes, but most of the time I never reached my destination without running out of gas. The truth is simple, if you don't have gas in the car your progress is completely halted. You're not going anywhere and you will more than likely be stuck on the side of the road, stranded. All because of a refusal to do something that was very easy, yet extremely crucial to your progress.

I don't know how many times I had to get out of my car and walk to the gas station. The whole time thinking to myself, why didn't I take the time to put gas in my stupid car? I wouldn't have to walk to the gas station and waste half of my day dealing with my lack of care. Many times, I was too much in a hurry, too focused on the wrong things to remember the basics priorities. It seems like a simple concept, no gas in the car equals me not going anywhere, versus, gas in the car equals I can keep going.

It's obvious that my car issues mirrored my life issues. My spiritual, emotional and physical tanks were all reading empty and I couldn't continue. Because of this pit of emptiness in my life, no progress could be made and everything came crashing down. I tried to start my spiritual engine, put on a good smile and make it to the next day, but that never lasted. My spiritual condition was getting worse by the day, my sponge was getting more and more dry. My wife's words were affirmation of my demise. My life was unraveling right before her eyes and I am sure it was heartbreaking for her to watch. I was focused on the wrong things, and failed in the areas that truly mattered.

No fuel meant no progress and no progress meant no family.

When I got my first car, my dad told me that I would have to do more than just put gas in it. If you don't put coolant in the car, the car will overheat. It was also never a good idea to drive your car around without frequent oil changes. Eventually a lack of upkeep and maintenance will shut everything down. My issues were not just a lack of fuel, it was deeper than that. There were several areas of my life that I had failed to maintain and because of that, everything came to a screeching halt!

How Did We Get Here?

How does one arrive at a pivotal moment like this in their life? How do you go from a family that was planting and pastoring a church together to a family that is being torn apart by the enemy? One thing is certain, it didn't happen overnight. It was a gradual and at times a very subtle process. It certainly wasn't a nose dive into danger but more of a drift into the darkness.

1 Peter 5:8 warns us about this: *"Be alert and of sober mind. Your enemy the devil prowls around like a roaring lion looking for someone to devour."*

The imagery of this scripture is vivid. I can imagine the enemy lurking in the shadows, ready to pounce on fresh meat in covert stealth mode. He is ready for us to leave room for him to slither in. That is why we have to take heed to the warning to be ready and to have a clear mind at all times. I admittedly failed to do that for a variety of reasons, none of which are valid but none of which were intentional. Unfortunately, life isn't built on good intentions.

My life had locked up like a car that locks up its brakes moments before running a red light. If the process of getting to this place was slow and steady, the final straw was quite the opposite. It was abrupt and a harsh reality to the truth.

To discover how I arrived at the most excruciating point of my life, we have to go all the way back to the beginning. Not to the beginning of the year or even to the beginning of my marriage, but back to the beginning of the issues that I faced. I had forgotten who I was and more importantly I had forgotten who I belonged to.

Back to the Beginning

My mother gave birth to me when she was 16 years old and my dad was only 17. Needless to say, I was far from planned. I grew up in the Bible belt in Chattanooga, Tennessee, although I have never owned a bible-belt, whatever that is. I am sure there is such a thing. It almost sounds like a championship belt for bible quizzers, which would be awesome! I was raised in a middle class home as an only child until I was 13 years old. I had a tremendous support system with amazing grandparents and a tight knit extended family. When my baby sister, Abby, was born, I suddenly didn't get all of the attention that I was accustomed to. You could say I was a bit on the spoiled side. My mom would go into debt just to make me happy and give me what I thought I "needed."

I had a great relationship with my mom. She was always there for me and she made sure we were always in church every time the doors were opened. She was a great model of a devoted believer that really taught me the basics of faith. Her family had a rich Christian heritage that went back generations. In the south, we have what I call "hand me down religion." We tend to pass down our belief system from one generation to another. For instance, if your parents were Baptist and their parents were Baptist, there is a good shot you were going to be Baptist. It's not just a Southern thing, it is that way in many families.

Our belief system isn't the only thing we tend to pass down, it also happens with our politics. When you ask most people, why they vote on one side of the aisle or the other, it's usually because their family voted that way. While in many ways it was blessing to have that rich heritage, it can also be a hindrance. While a great Christian heritage helps shape who we are, it doesn't mean anything when it comes to our personal relationship with Christ. Our belief system can be embedded in our lives at a young age, however, our salvation cannot be passed down from generation to generation.

We each have to discover what we truly believe and why we believe it. We make the choice to accept Christ into our heart. Our parents can't do that for us. It is a personal decision that each of us have to make.

I made that important decision to follow Christ at the age of nine. I walked down the aisle of the church by myself and made that life-changing decision. I was old enough to understand what it meant to accept Jesus into my heart, but I didn't have a full grasp of the seriousness of my decision. While I had a desire to follow Christ, I had no idea what it truly meant to be a Christ follower.

My mom was very active in the church, which in turn made me very active in the church throughout my childhood and teenage years. I liked church and had a genuine desire to grow in my faith and I also liked hanging out with my friends. I never had to be dragged out of the bed to go to church.

On the flip side, my dad was not a Christian and rarely went to church with us. So there was always a pendulum in our house that went from my mom, who was a fully devoted believer, to my dad, who wasn't really interested in church. My dad was a good man, he just didn't have a relationship with Christ and I witnessed him struggle with that lack of peace in his life for many years.

His struggle didn't just affect him. It affected the whole family and those around him. It created a strain on our relationship as father and son that would last for years. He was unaware this strain would put stress on future relationships that I would have throughout my life.

My father owned a paint and body shop and he was very talented in what he did. He was one of the best painters in town. When I was younger, he would leave our house at night and tell us that he was going to turn out the lights in his shop. He would be gone for hours and sometimes would stay out all night. There were several occasions throughout my childhood where my dad would be gone for days at a time.

I had so many questions going through my head as a child. The simplest question in my mind was, "how long does it take him to turn the lights out at his shop?" Of course my questions would gain more logic as I grew older. I never wanted to push the envelope because I didn't want to get in trouble. I didn't think it was my place as a kid to ask those questions. I was raised to be respectful of adults and grew up in an environment where we didn't always openly discuss complicated issues.

As a child, I viewed my mom as non-confrontational and at times I felt she just let things slide without being discussed. What I didn't understand at the time was that my mother did confront my father. She just did it in a different way than I felt she should have. She protected me and my sister from the arguments and handled her business privately. There were many times I could tell my mom was holding her emotions in, even though she was on the brink of breaking under the pressure and stress that my dad brought to our family.

The late nights and empty promises that my dad would make to our family began to build my animosity toward him and ate at my core. There were many times that I would be in a dugout getting ready to take the baseball diamond and I would look toward the parking lot to see if my dad's car would pull in. An inning would go by and there was still no sign of my dad. The game would be nearing the conclusion and I still had one eye glued to the game and the other eye waiting and holding out hope that my dad would care enough to show up. I may have only been nine years old, but I wasn't dumb. As a parent, I now know how kids are affected by our poor decisions.

Discovery

When I was 10 years old, I went to visit my dad at his shop. It wasn't often that I would visit him at work, but on this day I did for some odd reason. This was a day that will live in infamy. It would begin a ripple effect in my life for years to come. As most ten year old boys do, I liked to explore. I certainly would consider myself an adventurous kid. On that day, exploring meant looking through my dad's desk drawer to see what I could find. What I found was more than I bargained for and certainly more than a boy my age should ever have to experience.

As I cracked open the bottom left drawer of my dad's desk, I discovered for the first time, an adult magazine. As a pre-pubescent boy, this was devastating and intriguing and sickening all in the same moment. It was a rush of emotions and I immediately felt convicted. Something was certainly wrong in my soul.

I had already accepted Christ into my life, but I didn't have enough maturity to understand that sin was very real. I knew at that moment, this would be an issue for me in my life. I never told my dad and certainly didn't tell my mom. I kept it my dirty little secret for the longest time. This was my first encounter with pornography, but unfortunately it wouldn't be my last. It would return later in my life and play a part in damaging my integrity and eventually my marriage.

Short Fuse

Growing up I always had a temper. One of my earliest memories of anger came when I was in elementary school. My Mimi (grandmother) would pick me up from school every day and on our way home she would stop and get me a snack or a whole meal, depending on my hunger level. On this particular day, she didn't have any cash with her. Be reminded this was before the era of debit cards. We had to actually carry cash to purchase things, it was a crazy concept.

I wanted her to stop by a particular eatery with golden arches and a creepy clown that likes to hang out with other creepy characters like the purple blob and a bandit that steals little kid's hamburgers. They must have been giving something amazing in their kid's meals like the General Lee car from *Dukes of Hazzard*, because it wasn't my favorite place to eat and that remains true today.

Now there is one thing you need to know about my God-fearing Mimi, she is as gentle as a baby lamb. Some would say she is saintly, one of the sweetest ladies you will ever come in contact with in your life. Her personality is certainly meek and mild. While we were driving home on that day, she broke the devastating news to me that she didn't have any cash. She told me almost as if she was apologizing, like she was letting me down. Needless to say, I didn't take the news very well. I absolutely flipped out, blew a gasket and angrily told her in my childlike wisdom, "Write a check for it!"

Of course, she almost laughed at the thought of writing a personal check for a happy meal. Even though writing a check might have been a funny thought, there was a deeper issue here. Even as a child, I didn't like it when I didn't get my way. Life isn't like the other hamburger joint, we can't always have it our way. It would be dangerous if God allowed us to have everything we wanted. Our ways are not always best and most of the time, they are not the most beneficial.

1 Corinthians 10:23 talks about that, *"I am allowed to do anything"--but not everything is good for you. You say, "I am allowed to do anything"--but not everything is beneficial."*

We have free will to do what we please, but we have to realize that God, thankfully, doesn't allow certain things in our lives to protect us from ourselves. When we are told no by someone of authority, we can often get angry because we think that we have the greatest understanding of our own needs. Usually our "needs" are not a necessity at all, they are just our selfish desires. When our selfish needs aren't met in the way that we desire for them to be met, we are left with emotions that we can't control without the help of God, one of which is anger.

We have to realize that God isn't really concerned about our selfish desires. He wants to give us what we need in abundance. Most of the time our lack of patience prevents us from allowing God to move and for Him to provide exactly what we need and at the appropriate time we need it. If I would have waited 10 minutes until I got home, my Mimi would have made me a meal that would satisfy my hunger in more ways than any chicken nuggets could ever think about satisfying.

We have a loving heavenly Father that will provide for our every need.

Philipians 4:19 says *"And this same God who takes care of me will supply all your needs from his glorious riches, which have been given to us in Christ Jesus."*

Think about that, God gives from His riches and the last time I checked, He has an unlimited means and will supply all our needs. He not only gives generously but He is a God that loves to care for His children in ways that we can't imagine. At that point in my life, I didn't understand this concept and I began a pattern of selfishness, impatience and anger, a pattern that wouldn't be realized until much later in my life.

The Hole in the Floor

My anger issue became worse in my teenage years. It wasn't just my anger, it was my selfishness and this new character trait called arrogance. I was playing sports, was musically inclined and I began to date in high school. I was in ego overdrive and I still wasn't being told, "no" very much. My mom and dad disciplined me. I didn't like it and provided resistance as a way of rebellion.

I was also physically maturing and thought I was invincible. If I thought I was Superman, my dad was certainly my Kryptonite. As his life was spinning out of control, he was spending less and less time at home. He would throw himself into his work and he refused to allow his family to be a priority. He was fighting demons that we had no idea he was facing. My dad was in a dark place. We were left out of the loop not knowing what to do or how to help him. He needed to be rescued from this darkness and the only person to do that was Jesus. My dad knew who Jesus was, but he had no clue what it meant to be in a relationship with Him.

Unfortunately, at a very young age I was thrust into the role of the man of the house when he wasn't there. I helped out quite a bit with my baby sister because of our age difference. When I was 16, she was 3 and I felt the need to fill the gap for my father, who was absent most days.

Throughout this time of life, my resentment was building up against him. The difficult part was when he came home. He would be gone for days at a time and when he would come home he would act as if he had not missed a beat. He would pick up being the disciplinarian right where he left off. There lies the rub. No one wanted to address the elephant in the room. It's almost as if it didn't exist. We just simply ignored it. That elephant was simply a question. What was keeping my dad away at night and sometimes days at a time? No one wanted to hold him accountable for whatever was happening in his life.

When I was sixteen years old, my dad came home after being gone for a couple of days. He began to get on to me for something that seemed very minor. He was extremely upset and me being the "man" that I thought I was, I had the bright idea to challenge my dad to a fight. Superman, meet Kryptonite. My resentment had reached a new level. My mom tried to be the mediator but this time it didn't work. I spared my dad in the floor of our den like a WWE wrestling match. I pummeled my dad and the force of the impact left a hole in the hardwood floor beneath the carpet that is still there to this very day. No one was hurt physically. However, we both harbored so much hurt and regret.

I left after a few seconds, because I thought my dad would literally kill me. The relationship between us had become explosive. I was tired of walking on eggshells and I momentarily lost my temper and unloaded all of the hurt and pain. I had let the anger in my life take control of me. There were no fruits of the spirit present on that day. Not only had I let the enemy have his way, I blew my witness for Christ to my dad in that moment.

Every time I visit my mom in my childhood home, I walk over that hole in the floor and think about how ashamed I was and how much regret I have about that day. It also serves as a reminder of how far God has brought me in my life. The truth is anger turns into bitterness. It never pays and revenge is never worth it. Anger and bitterness permeate your heart like cancer. Anger in and of itself is neither bad nor sinful. It is a useful emotion when applied properly and reveals to us our true values. However, the enemy makes good use of anger and bitterness and we end up suffering because of it.

I love the scripture in Ecclesiastes that says, *"Don't be quick to fly off the handle. Anger boomerangs. You can spot a fool by the lumps on his head."* Because of my short fuse, it seemed like I had quite a few lumps on my noggin. I was turning out to be the fool. One Proverb says, *"a quick-tempered person stockpiles stupidity."*
Later in life, God would reveal to me that my anger wasn't necessarily because I had a short fuse. It was because I was harboring other sin in my life. There was disorder in my heart.

Anger was the byproduct of other things in my life that I was dealing with. Anytime there was disorder in my heart, anger would spew out of my mouth and in my actions. In some ways it was a manifestation of other sin that I was dealing with.

CHAPTER 2
SECRETS REVEALED

Now let me make this clear, I was a pretty good kid. I wasn't a complete disaster. For the most part, I did the right things but my rough moments, they were rough. I went to church, I was involved in everything and I was kind to most people in school. I did the basics, but there were several issues in my life that I would allow to linger around for years. I never dealt with them and I thought if I could ignore them, they weren't real. I thought if they just came to the surface ever so often it wouldn't matter, I could deal with that. I lived with the illusion for so long that I could control these things without the help of God. I felt like I had them under control and I was great. I would also begin to justify it in many different ways.

I would tell myself, "At least I am not an alcoholic or a drug addict," which just made me sound like a legalist. As long as I wasn't hurting anyone or hurting myself, it must be ok. I also used the justification of the church. I am attending church, I even sang a solo every once in a while, I must be good. I still didn't get it, my life had absolutely nothing to do with how good I was or how many boxes I could check off. I had no concept of what Christ had already done for me, I knew about the sacrifice that He made at the cross, but for some reason it wasn't real to me just yet.

After I graduated from high school, some of the questions that I had during my childhood about my father began to be answered. I knew that Stewart Johnson was my father, but I didn't really know who Stewart Johnson was. He always had a tough exterior and never let me into his world. He was guarded and I didn't know why. At times it was very difficult to even hold a conversation because I didn't know what to say to him.

It turned out that I didn't like the answers that I received. My mother called me one day and told me to come home because she wanted to talk to me about something very important. When I got home, she sat me down and told me that my dad had been battling with a serious drug addiction for a while. The truth came to light and I was so disappointed. Even though I had speculated that something was wrong with my father's erratic behavior since I was a child, it was still a shock. It created further heartbreak and confusion in my life.

The revelation of this news, hit me like a ton of bricks. It all made sense now, the late nights, the empty promises and even the anger. The sad part was, he was a good man most of the time. At times, he would do anything for people. I truly believe he had a good heart.

In 1993 a blizzard of epic proportions hit Chattanooga, where we lived. At least it was epic for the south. 21 inches of snow fell in a very short period of time. Over the course of that week, me and my dad went all around town taking people food, kerosene for heaters and became a taxi service for those who needed to get around town. I will never forget the joy my dad had helping the people in need. I didn't want that week to end. I had discovered a glimmer of a bond with my father and I did not want to have to go back to school.

He wasn't himself under the influence of the demon of drugs in his life. It had complete control over him and the only weapon that could break that stronghold was Jesus. This was a step that he wasn't ready to take and the addiction continued to eat at the core of who he was. He was a man that desperately wanted to do the right thing and be a better person, but couldn't conquer this beast of addiction that would wreak havoc in his life and our family.

Even though I had some of the answers to my questions, my frustration towards my dad continued. I thought drug abuse was so repulsive and it is, but at this point of my life, I still refused to view my own sin as repulsive or damaging. The truth is my sin and all of our sins are just as repulsive as my dad's addiction. It's a symptom of a much deeper problem. Like all sins, it's a heart issue. At the same time, drug addiction is just as forgivable to God as lying or spreading gossip.

When God looks at an addict, you might assume He's repulsed by the addict's sin. I don't believe that's the whole story. I believe He sees the broken heart beneath the sin. Jesus came to bind up the brokenhearted. Addicts are the most brokenhearted people I've ever met in my life. They have a desperate need to not only kick their habit, but truly see a sincere heart transplant.

In today's church culture, we have acceptable sins such as food addiction and gossip. We are quick to judge the guy who stayed out partying all night, but we are okay with the guy who is at the buffet table for five hours. We are not okay with desecrating the temple with the weapon of alcohol but completely fine with using a fork and knife as our weapon of choice. The moment we start classifying sins and looking down on sinners we become a Pharisee. If you remember the Pharisees were the same gang that put Jesus to death, but they thought they had it all together.

In Luke Chapter 18, Jesus tells an amazing story about the Pharisee and a despised tax collector. The two men went to the temple one day to pray.

The Pharisee prayed this prayer, *"I thank you, God, that I am not a sinner like everyone else. For I don't cheat, I don't sin, and I don't commit adultery. I'm certainly not like that tax collector! I fast twice a week, and I give you a tenth of my income.'* This is like the old "I don't drink, smoke or chew or date girls who do."

How many times in our life have we said, "At least I am not like them?" We say it so quickly without even giving our own sinful condition a second glance. That is exactly the posture that the Pharisee used to present his "prayer" to God. We tend to tell God all of the things we aren't doing to make ourselves look shiny and blameless.

We also tell God the checkboxes that we are filling in so we can get the glory. We do this without even once considering approaching God with a repentant heart. As Jesus describes this parable, He then shares the tax collector's prayer that followed the arrogant prayer of the Pharisee. The tax collector couldn't even lift his eyes to the heavens to pray because he didn't feel worthy. He adversely examined his own heart and found his own sin to be repulsive and dirty. He sorrowfully prayed, *"Oh God have mercy on me, for I am a sinner."*

Jesus closes the story in verse 14 by saying:

"I tell you, the sinner, not the Pharisee returned home justified before God. For those who exalt themselves will be humbled, and those who humble themselves will be exalted."

The next time you take out your flashlight to illuminate the severity of someone else's sin, be sure to focus the light on your own. I am thankful that God now gives mercy to the humble. I wonder how my life would have been different, if I had learned this truth earlier. However, I am grateful that it's never too late to learn what God teaches us.

Dysfunctional Perspective

You may be reading this book and saying to yourself, this guy's family was pretty dysfunctional. He must have grown up in Crazy Town. Others are probably saying, that's nothing, you haven't met my family. My point is not to paint the worst testimony I could paint, just to make a point. My goal is show you that life is messy and at times, dysfunctional.

Dysfunction is all about perspective. No matter which end of the spectrum that you fall on, the truth is most families have elements of being jacked-up. I was blessed to have a family that loved me no matter what. I was always cared for and provided for, at times abundantly. Yes we had elements of dysfunction but probably no more than the average family. The great thing is, no matter how dysfunctional you think your family is, God already knows and can still move and change lives. He can be the Father you never had, or provide the nurturing love your parents didn't have the capacity to give. He can give you the encouraging words that you never heard from your own parents or provide a sense of comfort and affirmation that you are walking down the right path. He fills the gap for every missing piece of your life yet at the same time teaches you out of the deep wounds of your past.

Tullian Tchividian said, *"God works through dysfunction. He uses dysfunction to show that His strength is made perfect in our weakness."* If you don't believe me, take a peek in the Bible. You will find story after story of God working in the midst of dysfunction, because life is messy and it has been since Eve decided to partake in a piece of fruit.

The first family on Earth was a prime example of dysfunction. It didn't take Adam and Eve long to begin arguing with each other. They played the blame game for their own disobedience. They ruined it for everyone when they took the fruit from the tree God told them not to. There was also a good chance they didn't have the "My Child is an Honor Roll student at Garden of Eden Elementary," bumper sticker on their mini-van. Their poor kids hated each other so much that Cain murdered Abel. And you thought your kids were difficult to handle. If that's not dysfunctional, I don't know what is.

How about Abraham and Sarah's family in Genesis? He lied about his wife and said that she was his sister, twice. Sarah would tell Abraham to have sex with her maid, Hagar, to see if they could have children. She ended up getting pregnant and had a son, Ishmael. Sarah would then get abusive toward Hagar because of her jealousy and then Hagar would take her son and run away. They also had a black sheep in the family, Abraham's nephew Lot, who ended up being a disappointment to the family. You can't make this stuff up. This isn't a new reality show, it's the word of God. There is a reason we see so much dysfunction and struggle in the Bible. It shows us that God can use imperfection and heartache to refine us.

Even through the disappointment and dysfunction in this family, God poured down His blessings on them. His favor was abundant. Abraham would go on to be extremely faithful, even after some difficult days. He trusted God so much when asked by God as a test of his faith, that he was willing to kill his own son. That is extreme obedience. So, don't worry if you look around your home and you see a mess, God can still use it for His glory and His blessings can and will flow in your life if you stay faithful. Grace cannot be earned but you will find that we serve a gracious God that loves us and gives us what we need every step of the way. He finds us where we are, no matter the circumstances, but also loves us too much to leave us there.

CHAPTER 3
BOY MEETS GIRL

In the fall of 1997, I made the journey from my home in Chattanooga to the "big" city of Nashville to attend Trevecca Nazarene University, a small Christian university in the heart of Nashville. During the first week of school, I was on a mission to meet as many people as I possibly could. Little did I know that week, I would meet one person that would have a major impact on my life.

I saw her from afar and could not take my eyes off of her. I was fixated by her beauty. I immediately turned to my roommate Derek and said, "That's the one. That is my future wife." I knew it in my soul. I didn't want to approach her because she was with a guy. I thought she was dating the guy, but I found out later that she was actually walking with her brother who also went to the school. Sometimes our perception is not always reality, thankfully that was the case this time around. I know this is strange, but I remember the pants that she was wearing, they were cool and edgy. They had brown and khaki patches all over them. She was unique, unlike any other girl on campus. She was an individual that stood out in the crowd and I was so attracted to that.

I finally got the nerve to ask what her name was and she said, "Tiffany." I asked her out for a date and to my pleasant surprise, she said yes! On our first date, I treated her to first class entertainment, our school's Homecoming basketball game. Following the exciting game, I took her to a five-star restaurant, at least in the southern part of the United States, the Waffle House. What was I thinking? It's a wonder she even called me back after that experience.

It didn't matter where we went there was something special about her. My first act of stupidity in this relationship was to tell her I didn't want anything serious. Once again, what was I thinking? She ended up dating someone else and I dated other people as well. I found out quickly that the field didn't compare to Tiffany. By the time I realized it, she was seriously involved with someone else and would eventually become engaged. I left school and came back home, but I stayed in touch with her. Periodically, she would send me letters to ask how I was doing. Something inside of us both knew that our paths would cross again, it just wasn't the right time yet. She finally discovered that the guy she was engaged to wasn't the guy that she was supposed to be with and broke off the engagement around Valentine's Day of 1999.

That summer, I connected with her again after I heard that she was single. I was so excited to hear the news but I thought there was no way in the world she would give me another chance after I told her I didn't want to date her exclusively. She once again surprised me and said yes. We began to date and it got serious, but she was fearful. She didn't want to get into a serious relationship because she had been hurt in the previous engagement.

She was scared that I would hurt her as well, so we were on again and off again throughout the fall but we both wanted to be together. At this point, I was madly in love with her and I knew I wanted to marry her. She had become my best friend in the world. I thought I had everything together in my life, my relationship with Christ had strengthened and during my senior year of high school, I had felt the call into some type of pastoral ministry. That was her heart as well and I knew it would be a perfect fit. I just knew in my heart we would make a terrific team in ministry.

She was so compassionate and that was so appealing to me, because I didn't have much compassion. I knew there was so much I could learn from her and we could learn from each other. At this time, she was working with inner city kids in Nashville. She had such a way with these precious children. I could tell early on that she was wired to do that very thing.

On April 28, 2000, not even a year after we started dating for the second time, I asked Tiffany to marry me and she said yes. We were so much in love, a love I had never felt in my life. Life was about as perfect as it could be. There were no obstacles. We knew that together, with God guiding us, we could conquer anything.

On August 5 of that same year, we were united together as one. What God brought together, let nothing or no one separate. We made a covenant with each other for as long as we both shall live, at least so we thought.
It was a beautiful wedding on a gorgeous, humid August day in Tennessee. It was absolutely, without a doubt, the happiest day in my young life to that point.

Everything in my world felt complete. I was 21 years old, Tiffany was 20, and we had absolutely no clue what we were getting ourselves into. I had my dream girl and we had our own apartment, two cars and a job as a youth pastor. I was so naïve at this point of my life. I had this notion that the work was over. Now that we were married, we could put it on cruise control and coast. Now that we were together forever, no more problems, right? Looking back, I had no clue what I was doing or what it really meant to be a husband. Unfortunately, it took a long time to understand this concept.

They say that you get out of marriage, what you put into it. In year one of our marriage, I didn't put much into it because I didn't think it was required. I thought my wife was there to serve my purposes. Sure I enjoyed the benefits of marriage, but I was beginning to understand this whole marriage thing wasn't a walk in the park. At times, it was really, really hard. I was struggling in so many ways to survive and my past sin became my present sin again.

The newness of marriage wore off pretty quickly and our baggage began to rise to the surface. I had tried to stuff it down during the courting process and the newlywed phase. I was lying to myself that it was under control and something of my past, but when adversity came my way the enemy reminded me. I had unresolved issues that I never dealt with in a proper way. I just masked them and thought they wouldn't return. However, I began to get angry again, this time at Tiffany. I would normally get upset about minor issues such as money or each of our families.

We were struggling to survive on my salary of $20,000 a year. I never had to deal with money issues before and I was terrible at handling money, which put the weight onto Tiffany. As with most marriages, the first year of our marriage was a struggle and I was turning into the person that I didn't want to become. I didn't want to disappoint Tiffany and I didn't want to morph into my father's example of manhood.

During the first few months of our marriage, Tiffany found some files on my computer that were from my past. It was pornography that I had saved before we were married. I was not looking at porn at that time, but it was yet another carry over into our marriage. I am sure Tiffany was thinking at this time, who did I marry? I had fear that she would leave me.

Once again, this was another previous sin that I kept hidden from her and it was so damaging. Let me remind you that marriage itself doesn't prevent unresolved sin from spilling over into our lives. We all have some sort of baggage that we bring into marriage, some more than others.

We think that marriage will solve our issues, however sometimes the stress of marriage boils our sin until it's overflowing to the surface. The truth will always be revealed. If you are thinking about getting married, deal with your junk before you enter into a lifetime commitment. Let God truly heal your sin, before He has to heal your marriage. Sin that is carried into a marriage is magnified and multiplied when the marriage takes place. Don't misunderstand me, the healing process isn't a quick fix, and more often than not, you have to cope with lust in various forms, so you develop maturity in handling it. It doesn't necessarily just "heal" in a few premarital counseling sessions.

You may be saying right now, she won't marry me if she knew who I really was and she saw my sin. I get it, our sin is ugly and at times, really shameful but if she is filled with love and grace she can accept you, baggage and all. I'm extremely thankful that through God's grace, He accepts our baggage and forgives us completely.

In Matthew 12, it says there is *nothing* done or said that God won't forgive.

Nothing is one of those words that is all encompassing. It has no bounds. You may be thinking, my sin is too awful or my list of sins is too long. The word of God says it doesn't matter. He will forgive the deepest, darkest sin and the longest list of sins. That is extremely reassuring and it gives me everlasting hope.

Giving your mess over to God will also mean the world to her if you are dealing with these issues now rather than later. That will show her that you are willing to do whatever it takes to be a new creation in Christ in your marriage. The freedom that you will have from unloading the baggage before the wedding will give you the peace that you will need for a long lasting marriage. So as Barney Fyffe says, "Nip it in the bud!" Take care of this immediately before it does further damage in your life.

If you are already married, don't think the boat has passed you by, today is your day to reveal and release your baggage. Admit to your spouse today that affair that you have been having or the fuzzy math that you calculated on your taxes. Reveal your stash of porn that you have been holding on to since you were a kid. Tell him about the credit card tab that you ran up over the course of years. Yes it will be painful, yes it will cause hurt feelings, yes trust will be broken but the further you let it go the worse it becomes.

Today might be the most painful day of your life but it just may save your marriage and keep your family together forever. Don't wait until tomorrow, because you will continue the cycle, take action swiftly. Come clean to God and come clean to your spouse. Remember when you made the covenant with your spouse, it was made with God. The three of you are in this for the long run. You may be fooling your spouse, but you are not fooling God.

1 John 1 says, *"If we claim that we're free of sin, we're only fooling ourselves. A claim like that is errant nonsense. On the other hand, if we admit our sins—make a clean breast of them—he won't let us down; he'll be true to himself. He'll forgive our sins and purge us of all wrongdoing."*

John Calvin said the human heart is a factory of idols. Smash one, you'll create another.

It's not just about eliminating sin in your life or behavior modification. We must get deeper into the root of sin. You can clean up ALL these sins outwardly, but if the root issue in the heart isn't dealt with, new addictions, new bad behaviors will take their places. A total heart change is required. Look at what heart issues are driving you to act in certain ways and then allow the Holy Spirit to meet you there. That's when true change begins.

CHAPTER 4
TWO PLUS ONE

I was in the midst of my first ministry position as a youth pastor in Georgia and life was moving along at a breakneck speed. Only 5 months into our marriage, my wife and I found out that we were having our first child. We were so excited and I was a bit shocked, even though I probably shouldn't have been. We were doing nothing to prevent a pregnancy. I knew immediately that Tiffany would make a wonderful mother, she had tremendous motherly instincts. She loved other people's babies and I knew she would love and care for our child in an amazing way.

As for me, I was scared to death. I was already feeling inadequate as a husband, imagine what I felt when I heard I was going to be a father. The weight of the responsibility was almost too heavy to think about. I just wanted to do the best I could.

I immediately reflected back to my absent father and how I somehow had to outdo that performance. I began to overcompensate in certain ways. For instance, I don't recall my father showing much compassion toward me or even using words of affirmation such as I love you or I am proud of you. I began to tell my wife that I loved her frequently. At times, it was too much. I only tried to do the opposite of what was modeled to me. I learned what not to do from my dad, but then I went overboard. The news of a baby was exciting but a daunting responsibility. I was 22 years old and I was ill-equipped to be a dad, which of course most people are at that age.

Tiffany was sick most of the pregnancy and I did my best to take care of her. I would bring her tomato soup and an industrial size jar of kosher dill pickles. Pregnant women sometimes have the strangest cravings. Husbands of pregnant women begin to get cravings for some reason as well. I began to crave Wendy's hamburgers, but for some reason those cravings only took place at two in the morning. I suppose I was preparing myself for the lack of sleep that I would go through with a newborn baby.

I attempted to pick up the slack of household chores, which I was very inept at doing. I never learned how to do much around the house when I was growing up, but I did what I could. I am sure I failed miserably in many areas during those days with the laundry, keeping the house clean and cooking. I never took home economics in high school and believe me, it showed.

One day, during the second trimester of the pregnancy, we went for a routine ultrasound. We were so excited to see our baby and hear the heartbeat. However, our genuine excitement very quickly turned to worry and tears. Needless to say, we were not prepared for this "routine" visit. As the X-ray tech showed us the baby on the monitor, she suddenly discovered something that none of us were expecting.

I saw her face go from joy to "oh no, something is not right." She looked at us and said, "wait right here, I am going to get the doctor." Tiffany and I looked at each other with fear in our eyes, we knew something was wrong. A few moments later, the doctor walked in the room and began to scan and confirm what the X-ray technician had feared. The doctor looked at us with a very serious, concerned face and told us that our baby girl has what is called gastroschisis. It is a rare condition where babies are developed and born with a hole in their abdominal wall causing their intestines to grow on the outside of the baby's body. We had never even heard of this condition. Of course when the doctor broke the news to us, we both freaked out. There was a massive cloud of confusion and stress that hovered over us and a wide range of emotion filled our hearts. At the very same time, God gave us a peace that He would never leave us through this pregnancy. We were assured that God's hand was gently placed on our baby girl.

The verse that was our rock during this season of our life was Tiffany's favorite scripture,
John 14:27:

"Peace I leave with you; my peace I give you. I do not give to you as the world gives. Do not let your hearts be troubled and do not be afraid."

During this journey God gave us a peace that doesn't come from any other source, but Jesus. There was no doubt that we would need every drop of God's supernatural peace to get through this and He gave it to us. The Holy Spirit was so tangible during this journey in ways I had never witnessed before in my life.

We were immediately sent to a specialist to discuss what the next steps were. The specialist explained that this type of condition would require extensive surgery immediately after birth to put the intestines back into the abdomen. We were also encouraged by the doctors that more than likely our baby would be able to make it full term. That was a prognostication that wouldn't come to fruition. We were in for the roller coaster ride of our lives.

Planes, Trains and Angels

On August 11, 2001, Tiffany was 31 weeks along and I decided to take a trip to lead worship at a revival in the Dallas area. That sounds like a great idea, right? I mean the doctor did say that the baby would be full term. We had nine weeks to go and I felt it was a safe gamble to go and minister in Texas. When I woke up that morning I had no idea what kind of day I would face. It was mid morning in Texas and I was at a water park, yes a water park with my brother-in-law's youth group. I called to check in on Tiffany and the baby and she told me that after breakfast she couldn't feel the baby kicking. The specialist had told her to count the kicks after every meal and that morning, the count was at zero. It was an alarming sign, but we were hopeful everything was alright.

Just as a precaution she was going to the hospital just to have them check her out. Tiffany's parents were driving her to the hospital and she told me she would call once she found out something. I felt so helpless being so far away. This was on a Saturday and I had previously planned to fly back home on Monday.

As a frantic prospective dad does, I paced back and forth and I kept calling Tiffany to check on her. She finally called back after an hour or so and said that they ran some tests and discovered that she had an infection and it was harming the baby. The doctors advised that they needed to take the baby in the next 24 hours, if they didn't, both Tiffany and the baby would be at risk.

I was told to hop on a plane ASAP and get back to Chattanooga. I immediately called and worked out the flight situation, at the same time my mind and emotions were running wild. I knew I had to be calm for Tiffany and the baby.

45

This was go time, it was really happening and it felt completely surreal.

I made my way to the Dallas-Fort Worth International Airport to catch my flight. It seemed like the enemy was putting obstacle after obstacle in my way. From getting a ride to the airport, to finding flights, to not having a cell phone, nothing seemed to go as planned. I felt like I was going against the grain. However, I was not be shaken by it. Every obstacle that we face in our life, God has an answer and He always makes a way.

When I arrived at the airport, I ran up the escalator and stood in line to check in. After waiting a few minutes, I was told at the gate that the airport was being shut down because of a major storm. The skies began to darken and the clouds emptied with a torrential downpour. I couldn't even see the plane that was right outside the window.

After about an hour and a half, the storm cleared and I boarded the plane for Atlanta and from the ATL airport, I would catch a flight to Chattanooga. When I arrived in Atlanta, my gate was in a completely different terminal and at the very last gate. I didn't have much time to change planes, so I took off in my flip-flops and ran through the airport. I felt like Jack Bauer going to diffuse a bomb to save the world. I wasn't going to miss that flight! I made it to the counter with time to spare.

That is when the non-compassionate airline worker looks at me smugly and says, "Sorry sir, your flight has been cancelled and there are no more flights tonight."

At this point it was almost hilarious, I would have to rent a car and drive the rest of the way. Before I did that, I wanted to call the hospital and check in for a report. I went to the nearest pay phone, yes for some reason I didn't have a cell phone at that time. My Mimi (yes, the lady that didn't write a check for the kid's meal) answered the phone. She said, "Congratulations, you are the proud father of a beautiful baby girl." I began to bawl right there in the airport, there were people that turned to stare at me, but I didn't care.

First and foremost, I was happy that everyone was ok. On the other hand, I was disappointed that I missed something so significant in my life. I knew I would never have another chance to see the birth of my firstborn. The doctors didn't have a choice, the infection was getting worse and they had to take the baby immediately. Tiffany was doing well and the baby was heading into surgery. Jada Lynn Johnson, our firstborn, came into the world right after 9 pm on August 11, 2001.

I then ran another 2 miles, caught a train and finally made it to the rental car stand. I got in the car and put the pedal to the floor, NASCAR style. Needless to say, I went just a wee bit over the speed limit. I know without a doubt that God put a hedge of protection around our whole family that night. I was guided by Him to safely arrive in Chattanooga.

I finally made it to the hospital after 11 pm. I ran through the lobby, caught an elevator and went straight to Tiffany's room. We immediately began to cry and embrace each other. This was our first traumatic experience that we had faced together. I felt in some way I had let her down by not being there, but of course, who could have predicted that the baby would come nine weeks early.

After a few minutes, we got word that Jada was out of surgery and I made the walk down the hallway to see her. The nurse took me back to the NICU, where I would lay eyes on my very own child for the first time. I will never forget that moment in all of my life. I turned a corner into the pod where she was in an incubator and she was connected to every tube and line imaginable. She was the most beautiful two pounds and thirteen ounces that I had ever seen. I just stared at her, couldn't take my eyes off of this precious miracle from God. The love I felt for her was a love that cannot be described. I was now a daddy and it was real.

The doctors were able to put Jada's entire intestines back into her abdomen. She stayed in the hospital for seven weeks and today she has no lasting effects from her condition. She is now a vibrant, beautiful middle schooler that loves to surf, play volleyball and is quite the social butterfly. She is a special young lady and I couldn't be more proud of her.

Nothing about this pregnancy was normal. What is normal anyway? Most things that God ordains are not normal. If something is normal in your life, more than likely it's because things are going the way you had planned them. Very little during this season of our lives went as we had planned. We had planned to have a "normal" pregnancy without serious complications. We had planned that our baby would go full term and be completely healthy. We also planned to be in and out of the hospital in a matter of a couple of days, not seven weeks. We had planned for me to be there by Tiffany's side telling her to breathe like they do on TV. However, God had other plans.

We didn't understand the trial in the midst of going through it, we rarely do, but we understand that now. God has allowed us to share Jada's testimony with thousands over the last 12 years. Jada has a tremendous testimony of God's faithfulness and grace. God is always faithful, even when our script is rewritten to create an even better story. You may question His story and the reasons why He chooses to create something different. We have to keep in mind that He does it because He loves us and wants what is best for us. We have to remember that this type of hope isn't found in the outcome or result, but our hope is found in Jesus Himself. He is our only hope.

We are usually the worst judges of ourselves and we create the wrong story. So the best thing to do is to forget our plan, give God a blank canvas and tell Him to create a masterpiece. So far in the history of mankind since God created the sun, moon, stars and everything else, He has never created something mediocre. God doesn't do mediocre, He wants the best for His children.

I heard Pope Francis say recently in his homily, "Do we let God write our lives? Or do we want to do the writing ourselves?" Sometimes we have to allow God to disrupt our plans to see the greatest movement in our lives. We easily forget that God always has our best interests in mind.

You have probably heard Romans 8:28 on repeat in your church, "*And we know that in all things God works for the good of those who love him, who have been called according to his purpose.*"

This doesn't mean that trials do not happen to people who love God. He promises that even the trials can be used for our good. Sometimes, we are too busy questioning God to see the good. Whatever it might be that we are questioning, it can still be good because God is guiding us and He is good. As long as we can keep our eyes focused on Him and not our circumstances, we can make it through the times that go unplanned!

In the midst of the seven-week hospital stay for my daughter, our family's stress was multiplied. The unplanned events kept flowing our way. At the most inopportune time in our life, I was told by my pastor/boss that he was letting me go. This was my first ministry position and I was already being introduced to the ugly side of ministry. The church didn't offer any severance package other than a love offering on the next Sunday and my last paycheck.

The youth group that we were leading had grown exponentially both spiritually and in numbers. However, the vision of the church began to shift toward a daycare and preschool. They wanted to hire additional staff to support this vision. Youth ministry wasn't a priority, so I was let go.

I was told that I would need to resign and if I told anyone that I was forced to resign, our family would not receive the love offering.

Even though, we were hurt by this decision and the timing of it, God had a plan. It would be yet another trial that would draw us closer to Him and force us to rely more and more on His strength and power. That same week, Jada was finally healthy enough to be released from the hospital. We were new parents, trying to figure out how to take care of a premature baby who was recovering from surgery while we were packing up boxes to move in with my in-laws until I could find a job.

I was not prepared for this situation at all and was a bit on the demoralized side. As a man and a father, you want to do whatever it takes to provide for your family. As men, it is discouraging when we can't do that adequately. This certainly humbled me, at least momentarily. This season of life was our first landmark challenge and while it was tough, this season was the breeding ground to make us stronger. We would go on to say that the worst possible situation turned into the best thing that had ever happened to us. We were able to make it out of the grind on the other side better than we were before. This first obstacle tested our faith and stretched us to be stronger. It was the preparation ground for things to come.

CHAPTER 5
TRANSITION & TEMPTATION

Transitions aren't always easy. In fact, they can be painful and confusing. We were fortunate after I lost my job and the birth of our child, that we had a place to go. The support for our young family was nothing short of amazing during that transition. The love and care that was poured out by both of our families was simply remarkable. For those next couple of months, we would live with Tiffany's parents. Looking back, it was a great environment for us to be in during that transition period. It also gave us great support for our newborn baby who required special care. Two months later in December 2001, we moved to the Nashville area, where we would stay for the next seven years. I found a job working for a music company and traveled to churches on the weekends to minister through leading worship and speaking. We went through a season of healing over the next year after our traumatic ordeal. There was a desperate need to grow in our faith and grow closer to each other and we did. We celebrated some wonderful memories over the next few years and began to serve at a local church leading a small group.

This was a season of tremendous growth and the first time since we were married that we built true community with others. Through leading a group, we made friendships that would change our lives. We not only built relationships but we were beginning to truly invest in discipling others. We learned the value of community. It was much easier to go through life when you were sharing it with others. That doesn't mean that doing life together with others makes you immune from sin but it certainly provides you a support system around you when you do go through trials and heartbreak.

That is the essence of what the church should be, not masking the pain but revealing it and healing through it together. We saw this take place within our small group time after time. I remember throwing out the lesson many times, because we would deal with issues that the group was facing. Some weeks it was marriage issues, other weeks the conversation would shift to parenting. We were figuring out life together and helping each other through the difficult moments.

One of my favorite books in the Bible is James. It challenges me with hard hitting instruction. I should probably read James every Monday morning before my week starts to be reminded of the truth that comes from God's Word.

In James chapter 5, it says *"Make this your common practice: Confess your sins to each other and pray for each other so that you can live together whole and healed. The prayer of a person living right with God is something powerful to be reckoned with. Elijah, for instance, human just like us, prayed hard that it wouldn't rain, and it didn't—not a drop for three and a half years. Then he prayed that it would rain, and it did. The showers came and everything started growing again.*

Something special takes place when we come together as friends, confess our sins to each other and genuinely pray and care for each others. God answers prayers and the favor of the Lord falls on each of us.

At this point of my life, I was seeing God pour out His blessings on our family. In the fall of 2003, we bought our first house and discovered that we were expecting baby number two! We were so excited that we were having another baby and this time it was a boy. After Jada's unconventional birth and condition, we were praying for a healthy and uneventful pregnancy and delivery.

This time around, Tiffany went full term and gave birth to a perfectly healthy and chunky baby boy. Of course after our precious Jada, anything would have seemed chunky to us. We named our little chunk, Skyler Cole. I was thankful that I had the opportunity to be there for the delivery of our second child. I was holding Tiff's hand the whole way cherishing every second.

Our first child prepared us for our second. We were ready for just about anything. God has a unique and sometimes frustrating way of preparing us. He uses traumatic experiences in our life to prepare us for our future. Some of the greatest lessons in life are the most difficult to learn. It certainly makes you aware of the possibilities going into the next phase of life. We were more prepared for our wild and adventurous little boy. We had no idea we would experience events like Skyler locking himself in the bathroom and having to call the fire department to get him out. Maybe we weren't expecting it, but we felt more equipped to handle it when it happened. God always knows how to prepare our hearts for what's next, even when we think we are not ready for it.

We were blessed to have so much joy in our lives, but of course this didn't go unnoticed by the enemy. Sometimes when we settle into life, our guard comes down and it gives the enemy a foothold. Satan shouldn't get all the blame, we also make poor decisions and have no one to blame but ourselves. It is easy to blame the enemy, but we must take responsibility for opening the door for the enemy to come into our home. You wouldn't let an intruder who could do severe harm to your family into your home, would you? Satan is no different. He is out to steal, kill and destroy, what makes you think he won't try to destroy you? There is a difference between preventing an intruder from entering your home and leaving the door unlocked .

After our son, Skyler was born, things were going great but I slowly began to let my guard down and didn't put the proper safeguards in place. I didn't protect my home like I was supposed to be. Let's face it, when we think we have conquered something, we tend to get so over confident that we think it could never happen again. I felt that way with the temptation of lust and porn. If I wasn't dabbling in it, surely it won't return. We begin to think to ourselves, we won that battle and it's over. This is an act of arrogance.

The problem was, I wasn't openly inviting sin into my life, but there were certain safeguards that I thought I didn't need any more. Even when we are strong in a certain area, we shouldn't be foolish enough to let down our guard. Oswald Chambers says that *an unguarded strength is a double weakness. It gives the enemy the opportunity to drain your strength.* We become vulnerable and weak when we leave the door unsealed and unlocked.

One weekend, Tiffany and the kids went out of town and I stayed home because of work. In a moment of weakness I reverted back to an old cycle. I didn't have any safeguards in my life and that was my downfall. None of the child locks were activated on my TV and that opened up the opportunity for the enemy to slip in. I made a bad choice of purchasing an adult program that evening.

When Tiffany came home, she discovered my purchase and confronted me about it. All of the memories and fears that she had earlier in our marriage were rising up inside of her like a volcano. I saw the sorrow and disappointment in her eyes and I had a decision to make, I could be a man and admit that I made a bad decision or I could lie about it and try to get away scott free.

To make matters worse, I decided the latter and that decision was even worse. I was digging my hole deeper and deeper by the minute and there was no escape. I'd somehow forgotten a simple, yet concrete fact that God always reveals the truth.

My pride was so thick and stubborn, there was nothing that would break through it. A moment of lust and sin led to dishonesty and dishonesty led to stubborn pride. That was not a good combination for success. In fact, it was a recipe for disaster. My lust, arrogance, pride and dishonesty were returning out of nowhere. I feared failing my wife and family and also being looked at in a negative light. I knew that this wasn't me, this isn't who I had become. One moment of weakness tarnished so many good things I was doing.

I remember those couple of days being very dark. I was still refusing to admit that I was wrong and that I had royally messed up. Finally, after a few days, I came to my senses and admitted my sin, asked for forgiveness and did everything I could to repair the damage. The fallout was much worse because of the cover up. It always ends up that way. If I would have been honest in the first place, I wouldn't have gone through as much heartache. This is a lesson that I wish I would've learned right then and there. Unfortunately it would take much more to realize this simple truth.

The Porn Epidemic

I fell back into the trap of lust because I never really dealt with the issues of my past. I was only masking the issue and ignoring it. I was so arrogant to think I could handle this issue without putting the right safeguards around me. In today's culture we are experiencing a porn epidemic that is spreading more virally by the minute. If we think it's not destroying families and communities, then we are asleep at the wheel. It's time to wake up to this issue. Forty million American adults regularly visit porn sites. Internet sites alone rake in over five billion dollars per year. That is billion with a B, which is a lot of cash.

Some of you are saying, yes, that is a terrible problem for men. Think again, it's not just men. One out of three users are female and one out of six women are addicted. You may be saying to yourself as you read this, "Those people need to get in church." Here's the problem, the church has a pornography issue as well. 47% of Christians said that pornography was a major issue in their home. Convinced yet? How does the fact that the highest amount of users on adult sites are between the ages of 12-17 sit with you? If you recall, my first experience with porn was at the age of ten, very close to that age range. It is affecting every person in the household.

There are more people than ever struggling with this issue because it is more accessible than ever before. When I was a kid, we didn't have the easy access to such things. It was completely in the dark and secretive. Now you can access it from anywhere in the world via your iPhone or iPad. It also has become mainstream and more acceptable. I believe it's because we have become desensitized in our culture, we have blurred the lines of what is acceptable.

In the church bubble, we refuse to talk about this issue, it is simply taboo. Only the bold, fearless leaders like Ed Young, Craig Groeschel and others have exposed these truths in their churches and they have seen tremendous success in healing marriages and families. What's crazy is they have received flack over talking about sex and porn mainly from other churches and pastors. The sad news is other pastors are hesitant to dive into a topic like this. Some don't want to scare away their congregations, so they sweep it under the rug and act like it doesn't happen.

Hey pastor, just because you refuse to talk about it, doesn't mean the problem goes away. While you are refusing because of offending someone or the fear of being irreverent, there is someone sitting in your church on Sunday that needs to hear that they can find freedom from this addiction. In all fairness, I am preaching to myself as well. I was one of these pastors. I was too afraid to be transparent with my congregation, too afraid to let them know that I had struggled with it in my past. I even did a series called *Taboo* and talked about some of the issues in the church that we should be talking about. Knowing that I had dealt with this in my past, Tiffany urged me to preach about this and I refused. I was scared and too concerned what people would think. I still believed the lies of the devil, that I would lose credibility with the crowd. The biggest lie was that I couldn't be successful or effective while sharing my struggles and past.

This issue is serious, we should all be on red alert. Families are being destroyed, marriages are becoming fractured and children are being exposed just like I was.

How do we cure this epidemic, how do we stop the cycle? The Bible has scripture after scripture about the struggle with lust. God knew exactly where our selfish desires would take us. To stop this epidemic it starts with us. We need to take a look in the mirror and see that the problem starts with the person that is reflecting back to us. It starts with me!

James 1:13-15 says, *Temptation comes from our own desires, which entice us and drag us away. These desires give birth to sinful actions. And when sin is allowed to grow, it gives birth to death."*

Our desires apart from God can be so dangerous and can take us away from a close relationship with Him. Our selfish sin can even lead to death, spiritual death and even physical death. So how do we eradicate this from our lives? Here are some thoughts on combatting this epidemic.

1. **Blame-ology** When we are caught in sin, it's so easy to blame everyone else in our path, especially those in close proximity, namely our spouse or significant other. We use awesome excuses for our bad decisions, excuses like, "If you gave me more sex, I wouldn't have to do that." That is the worst excuse ever. It transfers the blame from you to her. Suddenly your sin is her fault, which is illogical. If we want to change this cycle, we have to grow up and accept the blame. I wish I would've learned this first concept so much earlier than I did.

There is not a good justification for our sin. The moment you try to justify it, no one buys it, especially your spouse. You lose credibility even more than you already have. Take the blame, it's your bullet to take anyway. Once we get blame out of the way, we can begin to allow God to heal the deep wounds that are inside of us. These deep wounds are all the reasons we find ways to self medicate and it's in the wound where God meets us for healing and transformative change. We can't just allow God to take away the pain and sin, but we must allow Him to give us the heart transplant that we desperately need.

If you're single, you may be telling yourself, 'it's okay, that's how I get by, it's just an innocent look' or 'I am not hurting anyone.'

Matthew 5 says, *"Don't go to bed with another's spouse.' But don't think you've preserved your virtue simply by staying out of bed. Your heart can be corrupted by lust even quicker than your body. Those leering looks you think nobody notices — they also corrupt."*

Don't play the blame game, take ownership of your poor choices to minimize further damage.

2. **Rip the Bandage-** The only way you can heal a wound is to rip the bandage off and give it air. I am not talking about airing it on Facebook or standing up in church on Sunday morning and admitting it in the middle of a worship service, telling people every issue known to man. I am talking about confessing it to your spouse if you are married. If you are not married, go to someone that you can trust with your life. Confession brings freedom in your heart and empties shame and guilt. There is nothing like lifting the weight off of your heart and releasing it. Don't rip off the bandage slowly. That is the worst thing ever. It causes more harm than if you just rip it off quickly. So, don't wait to rip off the bandage, do it today.

3. **Counseling-** Go to counseling immediately. Don't use excuses like "I can't afford it," find a pastor that will do it for free. They are out there in your community, I guarantee it. After I admitted my sin to Tiffany, I reluctantly agreed to go to counseling because of the stigma of counseling. I had always thought that if you went to counseling, something had to be wrong. I thought it was an admission of guilt and the sign that things are over and in a desperation stage. I thought it was a sign of weakness. I have now come to realize that counseling is a sign of strength.

If you are married, counseling shows you are willing to do what it takes to strengthen the bond of marriage. I strongly encourage couples to go to counseling together. When you got married, you became one. I have seen numerous couples who think they need space. It is fine to put up boundaries, but remember you are in this together. Even if one of you has an issue and the other doesn't, it affects the whole family. Go and seek God together, not always separately. If you are not married, seeking wise counsel is not a sign of weakness. It's the smartest step you can take. Unfortunately for me and my wife, that time around, we only went a few times and things seemed to be better. We both agreed that we were fine and didn't need to go anymore. In hindsight, I wish we would have continued to go. Counseling is crucial to the healing process.

4. **Safeguards**- I would rather be thought of by others as a prude, than to put myself in a bad situation where I may be tempted. I would encourage you to put every safeguard you can in place. Let your spouse set every password. That includes TV, phone, every computer and on social media. If your spouse is keeping anything off limits, that is a major red flag and an extreme cause for concern. Don't stop there, put filters and accountability software on every device that you come in contact with.

If you have a problem with lust at the gym, change the hours that you go or change gyms. I'm all for being healthy but don't lose your marriage, just because of your obsessive need to get buff. Buy a treadmill and a bio-flex (do they still make those?). If you pass the strip club on your way back home from work and that is a temptation for you, go the long way home. Don't put yourself in precarious positions that will not satisfy. It is not worth it. Some of these things are common sense, but sometimes when we are driven by lust and desire, common sense can be thrown out of the window.

5. Accountability and Transparency- Not only should you be accountable to your spouse. You should also be accountable to others. At that time of my life, I desperately needed one or two guys who would keep me accountable. After that failure, I had a group of guys that would meet at the Waffle House and we would ask each other a series of 10 or 12 questions. This was extremely helpful for me and for them. I am eternally grateful for those three guys in my life during that season, although I was still too ashamed to let them know I had struggled in my past. Even though I was answering the questions truthfully, I wasn't sharing about my past, which I now regret. I was too ashamed and thought those guys would judge me. Everyone needs accountability, but accountability is useless without transparency. I still had a shield up. I was still hiding my recent past. I couldn't have written this book without transparency in my life. I needed to forget about what people think and do what is right. I have learned that people will respect you more if you are real and raw with them. It may be messy, but it's the only way to truly live.

Pastor, you're not immune from this epidemic, in fact you are the prime target of the enemy. You have heard it said, the enemy likes to attack the ones that do the most damage to him. If you are doing great things for the Lord, you need to be on guard. In fact, if I were you, I would upgrade the security system. I am not talking about the security system that keeps intruders out of your house. I am talking about the security system that protects your family from the enemy's infiltration. Do what it takes to protect your marriage and your children from destruction. I have seen countless pastors that have had moral failures that began with porn and then meandered its way into the real thing.

Some of you may be thinking, I have sinned and God is finished with me, I am done. I am here to tell you that couldn't be further from the truth. God can still use you. Not too long ago, I met my friend Matt. His story proved that theory wrong.

Matt was on the fast track in ministry. He was married and had a three year old son. Everything was seemingly perfect for their family. Matt began to pour more and more of himself into the church and less and less into his family. His marriage wasn't at the top of his priority list like it had been previously and it sent him down a road that he wasn't prepared for.

As the hours slipped away from his family, he began to put less emphasis on safeguards and accountability. He had the arrogance that many pastors do, the arrogance that says, "I am a man of God and those temptations will never happen to me." I am stronger than that, we tend to tell ourselves.

Matt was disconnecting emotionally and physically from his wife. He was spending long hours away from home all for the cause of "ministry." Matt began to shift the energies that he had poured into his family to a female staff member. He was smitten and in a dream world that only existed in his mind. The two began an inappropriate relationship and Matt made plans to leave his wife and ministry to be with this other woman. They both were in a delusional state and no awareness of the consequences of their actions.

Through this ordeal, Matt lost everything that he once held dear to his heart. He gave into the temporary temptation that many men face and in exchange, he sacrificed everything that was real and pure in his life.

One night after he left his church and his wife, he was sitting in his empty, one bedroom apartment when God had His way in Matt's heart. At that very moment, God began the restorative work in his life and awakened his soul that had drifted to the dark waters.

Matt immediately desired reconciliation in his marriage, unfortunately, at this point, his wife didn't want to have anything to do with him. It was difficult for her to be in the same room as Matt because of the pain and hurt that she had suffered at his hands. She didn't want to talk to him on the phone and didn't care about any of the notes that he would send her.

After a long process of not giving up, consistently pursuing the desires of Christ and his wife, Matt's marriage was restored. Not restored to the way it was, but to a new place that he can't even describe. God didn't give him back his old marriage, He gave Matt and his wife a new marriage with the same person. The restoration that God did in Matt's life and marriage was nothing short of a miracle. His family was one again and better than ever before.

If that wasn't enough, God restored Matt back to ministry, where he is working for a thriving, healthy church. One of his responsibilities is helping men and women build dynamic marriages. This is just one of the many testimonies that God is using to build His church. God is not done with you, He has the same power to resurrect your story and give you new, vibrant life in your marriage, family and ministry. He finds ways to use people who have been restored with greater effectiveness than they had before their crash.

Temptation Never Satisfies

It was late one night when I heard a rumbling out on our patio. Earlier that evening I had put our garbage out there for some strange reason. I opened the blinds to our sliding glass door, turned on the porch light and saw something that was a first for me. There was a skunk ravaging through our garbage.

This little guy tore through the trash bag and scattered it over the patio. I tried to bang on the door to get the skunk to go away, but it was too concerned with our leftovers. One particular food group the skunk really enjoyed was yogurt. He loved it so much that the yogurt cup got stuck on his nose and mouth. We thought that was hilarious. Finally after destroying our patio, the skunk scurried off.

The next day, we were watching the news and heard that a skunk had a yogurt cup stuck on its snout. Our skunk had become a spectacle. I am sure the animal rights people really appreciated us aiding and abetting the skunk's yogurt habit.

Throughout my life, I have been that skunk. I believe more than just who will admit it, can relate as well. We constantly search for what looks good, feels good or whatever gives us pleasure. Sometimes it's even a positive experience, as I am sure that yogurt cup was to that skunk. However, in the end, they leave us more desperate and thirsty than ever before, craving what could never satisfy.

We get into a perpetual cycle, because the things we crave never satisfy our desires. I recall many situations where I wedged myself into something that I thought would bring relief or satisfaction. Many times that sanctuary is a trap, it's a deceptive offer. It's simply a lie. The best thing I have learned to do is flee from temptation.

2 Timothy 2:22 puts it this way, *"Run from anything that stimulates youthful lusts. Instead, pursue righteous living, faithfulness, love, and peace. Enjoy the companionship of those who call on the Lord with pure hearts."*

The only way to break the cycle of sin is to flee and make drastic changes. If you don't do something drastic, you may like your sin more than you think.

CHAPTER 6
THE GREAT UNKNOWN

Time would go by and we would remain on an upswing for a while. Every marriage has ebbs and flows. At times it's like riding an elevator, there are moments where we are going up to the presidential suite where life is really good and sometimes we hit the down button to the basement, where nothing good happens.

This was a great time for us, we were raising our kids, excited about the future and then God began to challenge us. We were at a crossroads in ministry and wanted more for our lives and we felt complacent in that area of our life. We really didn't know what the next step was for our family. We knew that God had gifted us in certain ways to be used by Him. This was a season of growth for me, it wasn't perfect, but we were certainly growing in Christ as a family.

I started to become the biggest church nerd ever. I would research churches, their systems and methods, their growth tendencies and I was getting some amazing ideas. More importantly, God was beginning to put a vision and passion in my life for the local church. I still had a bad taste in my mouth from when I was younger and on staff at a church, but now I was older and wiser, at least so I thought.

At this time, I was still traveling to different churches, but it was getting harder to leave my awesome family. For years, I tried to get Tiffany and the kids to travel with me. It was difficult to travel with two small kids. Little did I know, she had been praying about this. One day, she told me that she was going to start traveling with me. God was testing her obedience like God tested Abraham with Isaac. Sometimes He tells us to do something just to see if we will do it and then at the last minute, He shifts gears and provides another way. The gears were certainly being shifted in our family.

Tiffany and I went on a 21-day fast for the first time in our life and God revealed so much to us and gave us tremendous clarity. We were absolutely on the same page and knew that God was leading us back into church staff ministry. We were so excited about our newfound clarity and direction but it meant we would need to move away to serve. This meant we would have to leave our support system, amazing friends and a church that we loved dearly. This would be a much harder transition than we originally thought.

Freeze-Frame

Do you remember the show, Saved by the Bell? I loved when the main character, Zach Morris, would freeze everything in the scene and he would talk to the camera while everyone was frozen in time. I wish that I had those magical powers and this is the period of my life I would utilize those powers. In many ways I wish the book ended here but there were so many more lessons to learn. Have you ever felt like that in your life? If only you could freeze everything while you are on the mountaintop.

We love to go through the moments that are worthy of a Facebook status update, moments that you would not trade for anything in the world those seasons of life when you discover the sweet spot. We don't have the same appreciation for other seasons or moments we would never want to be captured on Facebook. They are the most painful times in your life. However, God has an amazing way of using the mountaintop experiences and also the times we are in the valley, to draw us closer to Him and make us stronger. So while it would be nice to freeze frame life, God allows us to live, love, hurt and keep moving forward.

Never Say Never

No, this is not a section of the book about Justin Bieber. It is about those times in your life when the words, "I will never," leave your mouth, followed by us telling God what we won't ever do again. After I was let go and burned in ministry, I said I would never go back into staff ministry. If you think about it, I was closed minded to the will of God. The church wasn't the one that hurt me. It was just a couple of people within the church. I had moved past it by this time and was assured by God this was the right direction. The only question was... where?

Earlier in my marriage, I remember my wife distinctively saying, I would never, ever live in Florida. Once again, it's funny we told God what we will never do. Since we both said we would never do these things, God chose to use those very things. We got the call to go on staff at a church in Orlando, FL. Our little family would be selling our home, loading up everything we owned in a U-Haul truck and making the journey to our new home in Florida. It's probably better if we never say, 'never.' God's scope is massive and we can't even comprehend the twists and turns of this life. He doesn't bother with words like never, impossible or can't. He is much bigger than never.

Too Good to Be True

We were only in Orlando for two months before we
discovered some issues with the church. The pastor had
become physically ill and the church was in serious financial
distress. By the time we discovered these problems we had
already bought a house and thought life was grand. Our
marriage and family were continuing on the pace we had set
before we left Tennessee. Life was busy, but it was
manageable.

We made the decision to homeschool our kids. Tiffany was
doing a tremendous job teaching them. However, the church
continued to decline and we were told that they would need to
cut our salary by 10%. We didn't have much wiggle room with
our finances but we knew God would provide. Pretty soon,
the pastor began to talk about staff cuts and further salary
deductions. I knew at that time that God was leading me to
plant a church. I prayed about it for a year to make sure my
motives were right.

I didn't want to plant a church just because things weren't
going well at our current church. I had to make sure it was
from God. Tiffany began to feel the affirmation as well. We had
always been such a great team in ministry and we were
certainly in one accord on this major decision. As we were
praying about it, we were told that the church would have to
fire two people. Fortunately, we missed the cut, but two of my
friends were let go. Even though I didn't get the axe, it only
put off the inevitable. I felt like I was on the Titanic after the
iceberg, it was only a matter of time before the whole ship was
under water.

During this time, Tiffany and I went through an extensive church planting assessment to see if we were good candidates to plant. A major portion of this assessment was the evaluation of our marriage. They told us that sadly, many marriages don't survive the process of planting a church because it is highly exhausting and extremely stressful. We were told it would test our marriage, so we needed to make sure we were strong enough to make it. We would end up passing the intense assessment with flying colors. At this point, our marriage was very strong and we moved further toward God's vision of planting a church.

After the staff cuts, we would then take another salary deduction. Our pay was now cut a grand total of 30%. Here we were, with a house on a fixed income and we were about to be like the rest of America, with a house that we could no longer afford. Around the same time, I told my pastor that I was planning on planting a church, but didn't know the timeline. Bad idea, it was like giving him an invitation to fire me.

It was just a few weeks later, he came into my office and said they had to cut my position. Go figure. I was leaving anyway, but I wasn't ready. I had no financial backing to plant a church and no other streams of income. We had zero savings and a mortgage that we were about to drown in. I had to face Tiffany and tell her that I no longer had a job.

At times, God prepares our hearts to receive challenging news. This was the case with Tiffany. We were both at peace because we knew God had something bigger in store for our family. We had grown so much since we were faced with the same news nine years earlier. Once again, God had prepared our hearts through an earlier trial. When you go through a scary transition in life, remember that this probably won't be the last one that you will go through. Try to learn and grow through it the first time and it will prepare you the next time around.

Planting a Church

We lost our job on a Wednesday and on Friday, our family went to the beach for the weekend with our close friends, Nick and Christy, and their kids. It was such an opportune time to get away, relax and pray for the next step. We were blessed to have great friends like this family. They completely encouraged us that weekend to take the leap of faith to plant a church. They wanted to help us make that vision a reality.

After that weekend, we had so much clarity about the direction to plant a church. The next Sunday, we met at Nick and Christy's house along with another family. We had six adults and six kids. That was our church. We would move to our home and we transformed our garage into a kid's ministry room. It was convenient because Tiffany was leading our kid's ministry. I was preaching and leading worship. A couple of weeks later, those two families along with another, came to me and Tiffany to tell us that they wanted to take care of us financially so we could make ends meet. We were so blessed to have amazing people who really bought into our church plant from the beginning. I will always be indebted to those original families. It is people like these families that make church planting happen. You always need people that are all in with the vision that God gives you. It's the difference between a successful church plant and one that isn't. You can have a vision and passion to carry out that vision, but you always need people that are going to champion that vision. That was what was happening with our church plant.

After two months of meeting in our home, we were running out of space. God was doing something really special within our core group of people. We were able to rent out the YMCA in the area we wanted to plant the church. It was a blessing from God how He opened up the doors. We would continue to build our core group over the next few months and saw some miraculous things take place. Our first major outreach event on Good Friday night drew over 1,200 people and we were expecting around 400. People were coming to Christ and we were making a solid impact in the community.

We launched the church that fall and we had a packed house the first week. Over the first year of the church, we saw numerous baptisms and the impact continued. We were adding families to the core of our church and we were building systems that would support our growth. Outwardly, everything looked great. Every week I did my best to paint the best picture that I could. Inwardly, I was numb and drained.

When I got to this point, my spiritual compass began to go haywire. My marriage was struggling. I was so focused on the church and "success" that I neglected the best thing in my life, my family. I was trading something from God for something that was good. When you trade a God thing for a good thing, you will get exactly what you bargained for. You will discover that good things don't compare to God's best for you. The church was becoming an idol to me. I was getting to the point where I was so focused on doing the work of the Lord that I forgot to focus on the Lord himself.

My prayer life resorted to selfish prayers and I would pray as needed. I didn't view prayer as building my relationship with Christ anymore. I took my prayer life for granted. I only read and meditated on the word when I was preparing for a sermon. All of these things that I let slip in my life, affected my family and damaged my marriage.

I started to take my wife for granted and we began to drift further apart. My attitude was such a turn off for my wife and the years that I had made positive deposits in her soul were gone. I was withdrawing more from her than I was depositing and I had become bankrupt when it came to her. I had gotten to a place where I know I was hard to live with and I know I was making her miserable. She prayed and held on. I was so blinded by my pride. Tiffany begged me to go to counseling but I refused. I thought there was no way she would ever leave me and I thought we would always be together. I was so stupid, I honestly believed that we could fix it, but she was tired of the cycles, the anger and the words that were cutting deep.

To make matters worse, our house was about to go into foreclosure. This caused tremendous stress on our marriage and stress on Tiffany. There are so many people that are dealing with financial stress. I was so naive to believe that if we did nothing, God would fix it. I would use God as an excuse to do nothing. Let me make this clear, God can bring you out of your financial circumstances, but if you think He is going to drop a million bucks on your doorstep, you will most likely be proven wrong. God requires us to do our part. Matthew 6:15 says, *If you refuse to do your part, you cut yourself off from God's part.*

Sometimes He requires us to do things that are hard, but God will bless your obedience. That means, you might have to take on another job or two to take care of your family. I refused to do it and that was the wrong decision. I didn't want to do it because of the lie of my pride.

I am convinced that most of our issues in life are directly related to pride. I believe the enemy loves to use the weapon of pride to make us believe something about our self that isn't true. We begin to believe it as truth. At this point, I didn't want help because I thought I had it conquered. That's pride. I refused to go to counseling, because of my pride. I wouldn't admit that I was ever wrong because of…my pride. When I would get caught in a lie, instead of revealing the truth, I would try to ride it out, because of my pride.

I believe there is also pastor pride. We have this fear that if anyone in our community of believers thought that we had a crack in our armor, then we will be less effective and less credible. I have discovered the opposite to be true. God likes to use broken pots, because the water oozes through them. People can relate to them. The misconception that pastors shouldn't ask for help is prideful.

We need to take pastors off of pedestals and down to the street level where people are living, where they can be most useful and effective. I don't think God wants perfection from us, I think He wants authenticity. I want to be a broken vessel that God can use over and over again.
I want Him to remind me daily of my desperate need for more of Him and less of Jeremy in my life.
One of the best examples of pride in the Bible is found in a parable that most of us know. The lost son, or the prodigal son as most people know it, found in Luke 15. It's simply a story about a young man who demands his inheritance and runs off to the big city. He blows all of daddy's money and struggles to make it on his own.

We have heard stories of people just like this. We have all played the prodigal at some point in our lives. In the parable, this guy was eating the pig slop and was homeless without anywhere to go. He finally humbles himself and decides to wallow back home where I am sure he was expecting his old man to bust his chops and tell him, "I told you so," but that didn't happen.

As the father sees the son from afar, he runs to him, wraps his arms around him and welcomes him home. He throws a feast for the son, puts a robe on him and gives him everything. Even though the son didn't deserve anything, his father gave him everything. It is a beautiful story of the model of God's grace to us. Even though we don't deserve anything, God gives us a rich inheritance of Heaven through the cross. We deserve death and Christ offers life. You are probably thinking what does this have to do with pride? It happens in the side story of the older brother.

Eugene Peterson writes it like this in The Message:
"The older brother stalked off in an angry sulk and refused to join in. His father came out and tried to talk to him, but he wouldn't listen. The son said, 'Look how many years I've stayed here serving you, never giving you one moment of grief, but have you ever thrown a party for me and my friends? Then this son of yours who has thrown away your money on whores shows up and you go all out with a feast!' "His father said, 'Son, you don't understand. You're with me all the time, and everything that is mine is yours—but this is a wonderful time, and we had to celebrate. This brother of yours was dead, and he's alive! He was lost, and he's found!'"

Even though the older brother had been given everything as well, he was still all about himself. He was blinded by his pride and what the younger brother had done to see his own sinful condition. He was too prideful to celebrate the very thing that Heaven was celebrating. The older brother was too consumed with fighting the wrong battle and he was focused on the principle that he missed the big picture.

I had turned into the older brother. I was too consumed with self, that I was missing what was truly important. Winning the arguments and the battles are not worth losing relationships. Pride is one of the biggest killers of relationships. If you are struggling with getting your way or being right all of the time, you more than likely have an issue with pride. Pride is sneaky because you don't realize you're struggling with it until it's too late.

In the generation of entitlement, we need to rely on God who has already won the title! The quicker we realize that we are not entitled to anything but God loves us enough to give us the whole world, the quicker we will find true peace and this alone can strengthen our relationships with others.

Full Circle

A few days before Tiffany's departure, there was a straw that broke the camel's back. There's always a straw. It wasn't the thing, but it was a culmination of my condition and years of frustration.

Pastor Steven Furtick says that, *Frustration comes when our expectations exceed our experience.*

One day in early December, I went to the beach for lunch without telling Tiffany and when I was asked about it, I lied about it, again. At this point, trust had already been broken, I had no credibility with Tiffany. My withdrawals from her far exceeded my deposits and bankruptcy was inevitable. I was done. I was at the end of my rope, completely drained of everything. When I finally admitted it, I blew up, threw a cup against the wall and stormed out. Tiffany evidently had enough. It was upsetting for her and Skyler, who was home at the time.

I was so ashamed of myself and I remember being so sick of me. I was literally disgusted with my life and I was shaken with emotion. Still too prideful to even admit it to my own wife, I knew something had to change because I was in the worst season of my life. None of it made sense to me at the time, remember, from the outside looking in, I had everything. However, the one thing I needed to facilitate the rest was Jesus and I had drifted so far from Him, even though He never drifted from me. My relationship with Christ was just a caricature of what it used to be. I didn't make time for Him and everything in my life suffered because of it. After my wife and kids left, I would begin an unexpected journey that would change my life forever. Changes are coming, but will there be a steep price to pay?

CHAPTER 7
SATURDAY

Let me paint a picture for you. Good Friday is over. The tomb has been sealed. Jesus has died and darkness and sadness fill the Earth. We all are fully aware of what took place on "Good" Friday and the darkness goes away on Resurrection Sunday, but no one ever talks about Saturday, the period between the darkest moment in history and God's finest moment of defeating evil and conquering death. Imagine being a disciple on that Saturday. This had to be the lowest moment of their lives. The Bible doesn't make much mention of the time between Jesus dying on the cross and Jesus defying death.

John 20:19 says that the disciples *"shuttered in fear and locked the doors behind them."*

They were understandably still in shock and scared senseless. They must have had so many questions, so many emotions and so many regrets. I am sure they re-examined every second of the last week of Jesus' life. Could they have done something to prevent His death? I am sure those thoughts went through their minds repeatedly. I would have had them and would have rewound every circumstance and every moment. The disciples were in deep sorrow and I would imagine that it was difficult to pick themselves up off of the ground after experiencing that traumatic event. The question that probably haunted their thoughts was simply, why? Why did God allow this tragedy to happen? Why didn't Jesus call the army of angels that were at His disposal to rescue Him from this situation?

Some of these questions had validity. There was such a mystery. They may have even felt like they would never recovery from it. What they didn't know was that the resurrection was on its way. That is a great reminder for all of us. It may be dark today beyond our wildest imagination, but joy will return in the morning. It may not be the way you think it will happen or in the timeframe you would like for it to happen. God's promises to Adam and Eve took thousands of years to fulfill. Israel endured decades in a desert, and later hundreds of years of silence before Christ arrived. God may never be in a hurry, but He is always on time.

The disciples had no idea the turnaround that was about to happen because they didn't have any perspective. We rarely do when we go through the struggle. We need to see it in the rearview mirror to gain a proper view of God's purpose. Only after the tears, after the pain and after the struggle can we begin to gain clarity.

Remember that when you look into a rearview mirror, objects are closer than they appear. Whatever you are struggling with, whatever you have gone through, the resurrection, the deliverance is closer than it seems. It may feel like at this moment that this pain is never going to end, but I can assure you, the turnaround is near. Some of you may feel that your addiction will never be conquered, but with God's grace, your freedom from addiction may be just around the corner. It may seem like your marriage or your current broken situation will always be broken, but I am here to tell you, God can resurrect your broken pieces.

I admittedly felt like the disciples after Jesus died. When Tiffany left, I had no perspective. I was angry but I also knew that I needed to change. I had some difficult decisions to make. I could keep being the same person that I was or I could allow God to do an overhaul of my life. If I chose to continue to be the same person, I would be committing acts of insanity because we all know that the definition of insanity is to continue to do the same things over and over and expecting different results.

I was at a major crossroads in my life and it was the darkest place I had ever been. Friday was over but now it was my personal Saturday. Now I don't want you to miss the point here. I am by no means comparing my situation, with the death of Christ and the agony that the disciples felt. I am simply saying that every person will go through at least one Saturday in their life. It's the period of time after a traumatic or life changing situation.

Most of the time, our Saturdays are seasons rather than just a single day. I heard Steven Furtick say recently, *"God schedules every season in life, but He doesn't post the schedule for us to see."*

Oh, how I wish He would, it sure would be easier. How I wish I could have seen the hard times before they came but that isn't how God works. Unfortunately for us, there is never an indicator of how long our Saturdays will last. One thing is for sure, Saturdays are important and are not to be discarded as just the hard season of life, it could be the season that shapes you to be the person God calls you to be. But that requires a decision. In our darkest hour, on our Saturday, the decisions that we make during this time could alter our lives forever. Many times, God uses our Saturday experiences to mold us through our suffering and pain.

Run to Him

One of my favorite decisions comes in John Chapter 11.

The moment she heard that, she jumped up and ran out to him. Jesus had not yet entered the town but was still at the place where Martha had met him. When her sympathizing Jewish friends saw Mary run off, they followed her, thinking she was on her way to the tomb to weep there. Mary came to where Jesus was waiting and fell at his feet, saying, "Master, if only you had been here, my brother would not have died." (John 11:29-32 MSG)

This passage is an amazing picture of how we should deal with our Saturdays. Mary and Martha just lost their brother, Lazarus and to be honest were not too happy with Jesus. They thought He could have saved their brother. Have you ever felt like that? Have you ever been so upset with God, that you didn't want to praise Him? In fact, you didn't want to hear anything that had to do with God. I can imagine Mary and Martha felt that way and they were as close as you can get with Jesus.

Mary had a decision to make, will she run to Jesus or will she run to the tomb? Will she run back to the tomb, where it was filled with death and was hopeless or would she run to the very person that embodied life and hope? Instead of dwelling on the tragedy and continuing to weep, Mary ran straight to Jesus and fell at his feet.

The scripture also says that Jesus was waiting patiently for Mary, such an amazing picture of God's grace and His steadfast patience. He is always waiting patiently for us to run to Him. Sometimes when we go through a situation that is tragic and brings us pain, we tend to run to that pain. We not only run to our pain, but we run to anything but Jesus.

We overanalyze it and our problem or situation becomes our idol. Rather than running to our pain, we should run the opposite way into the arms of Jesus.

When we run to that thing that brings us pain it never satisfies and we are always stuck mired into a cycle of pain. We look around and wonder, where is God in all of this mess that we are in? The answer to that question is simple, Jesus is always there with us, He hasn't gone anywhere. Unfortunately, we attempt to hold onto it as long as we can and try to control it and we try to manipulate it to make us feel better, but it never works.

We must come to a tipping point in our life. A place where we end and He begins, a place where He is always waiting patiently for us. It's called surrender. For the life of me I don't understand why we always wait to run to Him but I know that even in the interim when we are running away and trying to fix it on our own, He is still with us. He is allowing us to go through certain situations but He promises that He will walk through those with us. When we finally realize that running to the tomb rather than running to Him is not the answer then we can allow Him to work and move in our lives. That is the moment that we begin to see the blessings in our life. That is the moment that God plans the greatest miracles that we will ever see because of our obedience and faith. The faith that believes He can do those things, not us.

My prayer today is that we quit running back to the tomb to weep but rather run to Him, fall down on our knees because He's always been there waiting patiently for us and in Him we will find everything that we need. At this point, I was still in too much pain to realize my need to fall in His arms. I was ready to see changes but I still didn't see the need to surrender, but I would see it very soon!

Walking Through the Dark

My Saturday began on a Thursday. I had to experience the aftermath of my family's departure. My world had been flipped upside down, inside out. I remember waking up to the silence of an empty house. The sound of silence was deafening. I remember feeling a sense of loneliness that I have never felt before in my entire life. Tiffany's words from the day before were on a perpetual rewind in my mind and on my heart, I remember her saying that she "still loves me and she still wants to be married to me, but I needed to work some things out first."

I began to relive every moment of the past 13 years in my mind, which was sobering and stressful all in the same emotion. The guilt, the weight and regrets of everything I had become was almost too much to bare. The devil was working overtime in that house. The spiritual warfare was so heavy, that at times, I had to get out of the house and just pray to God. I would go on long walks or I would just drive around to clear my head and began to have conversations with God again. I would begin to talk to God more in one day then I would previously in a month.

I kept crying out to God, why? How? I was in complete agony and the frustrating part of it was that I could have easily prevented all of this. What I didn't realize at this point was that my wife and kids were also hurting. I wasn't the only one that was in pain.

I remember the next several weeks being extremely dark. I had very little communication with Tiffany, which almost drove me crazy. At first I thought this would be a short separation and we would be able to start counseling and we could fix all of it. Even through the darkness and shock of the first few weeks, I remained optimistic that we could reconcile everything. I still had some semblance of hope. Christmas was coming up and I still thought I could be with my family for Christmas but it became evident that the plans had changed.

That Christmas was one of the hardest things for our family. We had experienced every single Christmas together for the past 13 years. I decided to go back to Chattanooga to be around some of my family. The thought of being alone for Christmas was tempting, but it would have been even more depressing to do so. I remember getting up early that morning in my hometown and I went to my high school and just ran around the track, praying to God. I can't imagine what my children must have felt on that day, not to have their daddy there on Christmas morning for the first time. All I could think about was all of the great memories of Christmas past. The moments of joy in my kid's eyes I wouldn't get to witness that year was overwhelming.

I remember thinking that Christmas was supposed to be about the light of Christ and what I was feeling was completely the opposite. Even though it seemed I was walking through a dark room, the light was still there. As long as God is there, so is the light. Even when I didn't realize it, His light was guiding my path.

You may be reading this today and you may feel like you are in the darkness. Trust me, if Christ is in your heart, even if you feel distant from Him, even if you feel you have let Him down, Christ's light is shining bright. Just because your situation has dimmed, it doesn't mean the light of Christ has dimmed. We serve a God that doesn't fluctuate His light in our lives based on our turmoil or chaos.

Even though I felt the darkness, I still felt the warmth of His light and He was holding my hand and He never, ever let go. It reminds me of the Matt Redman song, Never Once.

Scars and struggles on the way

But with joy our hearts can say

Yes, our hearts can say

Never once did we ever walk alone

Never once did You leave us on our own

You are faithful, God, You are faithful

Let me be real with you, I wish I could've sung this song days after the bottom fell out, but in reality, I couldn't. There may be a period of time where none of this will make sense. It may be a period of just grieving. There may also be a time where there is self pity. I went through a period where I didn't feel like singing praise to our Father. You could even say I was bitter.

Immediately after the fallout, I still didn't get it. I didn't understand the gravity of my situation. At times I was so self-absorbed that I still thought it was all about me. I still didn't see it, I didn't have any perspective. I immediately went into fix it mode and thought I could still do it on my own. I was wrong in so many ways.

I remember writing in my journal days after this all happened, *" I am emotionally drained this morning, still in shock and I feel completely void of joy or love. I feel betrayed by the person that I love the most and never thought this would happen. "*

I felt betrayed because I was too blind to realize that she did what she thought had to be done. She was doing it to help me, but I couldn't see it. I firmly believe today, if she hadn't left, I wouldn't have made changes in my life.

We never anticipate the hard lessons coming our way. No one ever says, "Please God, bring me vast amounts of pain like I could never imagine, so I can make changes in my life and be a better person". We never invite the unthinkable to bring about good, however we serve a God that makes it a habit of taking what was meant for evil and using it for good.

You may be at the low point of your life and you are saying to yourself, I don't know how in the world there could be anything good that can come out of this. I want to encourage you that God can turn the darkest situation and breathe fresh life into it. You might have received some bad news from the doctor this week, I believe that even in your darkest hour God can reveal something special in you and through you.

God didn't cause your situation, but He can use it for your good and His glory. You might have to tell your wife that you lost your job and you can't even imagine how you will be able to make it another month. I am here to tell you that God can use this loss to bring about something good in your family's life. This may allow you to begin a dream that God has been leading you to for years. Either way, God can use it to bring about something special in your life.

Two days after my family left, I began counseling with a group that specifically works with pastors called Care for Pastors in Florida. I remember walking into the office a completely broken man. I didn't know who I was and I wasn't sure there was any future without my wife and kids. I was so confused and distraught. I was finally willing to do whatever it took to get my family back and get my life back.

The very first question that the counselor asked me was of course a trick question, at least I thought so. He asked me,

"Who is Jeremy?" I thought to myself, this is one of these deep, introspective questions like if you were a tree, what tree would you be? My answer was straightforward. I am a husband, dad, pastor, church planter, etc, etc. I began to describe the things I would associate my identity with, my personas, but those were the things I did, not who I really was.

The counselor stopped me quickly and said, "No, you are wrong." I looked back at him confused. I didn't know there was a wrong answer. He said, "You have been trying so hard to keep up with all of the hats that you have forgotten who you are. You have tried to become all things to all people and it doesn't satisfy." He then began to give me the real answer. He said, "Let me tell you who Jeremy is. Jeremy is a child of God, no more, no less, that's it."

When he told me this very simple answer, all of the pressures of the person who I was trying so hard to be were released. I could finally rest in knowing that at the end of the day, I am a child of the King and He loves me no matter what. I didn't have to pretend anymore, the stress was relieved.

After all these years, I was beginning to understand who I really was. My identity was found in so many other things and who I really was had been covered up. A mask was blocking the true me. I was finally content with just being God's child and His approval and love was all I needed. I know it's a simple truth, but I wonder how many of us have gotten lost in our titles and our roles that we have forgotten whose we are. We work our whole lives to become something, when in essence, the very person that God wants us become is just us. We have to come to a place in our lives where God is all we need because He is the only one who can fulfill. He is the only one that can truly satisfy.

CHAPTER 8

CHANGE CAN HAPPEN

It was announced to our church that I was going on a six week sabbatical and that I would return on January 20th. Little did I know on the day of the announcement, it would be my last day standing on the stage of a church that Tiffany and I had planted together. This was a church we had poured every bit of ourselves into, perhaps even too much.

The church was extremely supportive but they didn't fully understand the gravity of what was happening, I am not sure I did either at that time. Tiffany told me that she wasn't coming home and informed me this would be a long process, not a quick fix. I was devastated, but I knew that none of this was a surprise to God.

I would have to pack up the house and send all of our belongings to Missouri where Tiffany and the kids were staying with her parents. That was so hard to do. Packing up your kid's toys and clothes, knowing that this may be the last time you see those things, was difficult. God kept reminding me that these were just things and this was all part of the healing process.

In early January, I resigned from the church and moved back to Tennessee, into the house I grew up in. Talk about a humbling experience. That would begin a season of humility for me and that was a difficult thing to learn. I firmly believe that life change begins with humility. Someone once said, "Humility is like underwear, essential, but indecent if exposed." There is a good chance if you do not choose to humble yourself, someone will do it for you.

I knew that I needed a tremendous dose of humility in my life, because prior to this, I didn't have much. The sad thing is most people that desperately need humility, very rarely see the need for it. I had to be humbled and knocked from my perceived pedestal to have a desire for it. CS Lewis says, "Humility is not thinking less of yourself, but thinking of yourself less." God made it very clear, that His plan didn't revolve around my life. I had to very quickly discover that my life should revolve around His plan. Like a Christian song in the 90's said, "I was living life upside down." The moment we realize that we are not the hero of our own story and that Jesus is, is the moment we allow God's power to be activated in us.

During this season, I had a deep desire to look to Christ as the model for humility. My eyes began to be opened to His life and resurrection and what that meant for my life. If you really think about it, Jesus had a humble birth and an even more humble death. He embodied humility from the manger to the cross. If there is one thing I would like to acquire from Christ on a daily basis, it would certainly be humility.

If you are having a difficult time finding a consistent model of humility around you, look no further than Jesus. He is the blueprint of how you walk clothed in humility every single day. Imagine what it must been like to do life with Jesus day in and day out. What a treasure it must have been to have daily interactions with the One who was the most humble person to ever walk the planet. You have to think that being around Christ must have had a lasting effect on those around Him. We can have that same experience as the disciples by being around the things of Christ and developing our relationship with Him.

How do we do this?

In Philippians it says, *In your relationships with one another, have the same mindset as Christ Jesus: Who, being in very nature[God, did not consider equality with God something to be used to his own advantage; rather, he made himself nothing by taking the very nature of a servant, being made in human likeness. And being found in appearance as a man, he **humbled** himself by becoming obedient to death even death on a cross!*

He made himself nothing. I will admit, this is a difficult task. Especially in a world that strives so desperately to be *something*. It is the opposite of what Jesus did throughout His entire life. What do parents want for their children in today's culture? Parents want their children to make *something* out of their lives. Jesus is not saying that you can't be successful in your life. He simply desires our obedience and that begins with humility.

The proceeding two verses in Philippians says, *3 Do nothing out of selfish ambition or vain conceit. Rather, in humility value others above yourselves, 4 not looking to your own interests but each of you to the interests of the others.*

I had gotten to the point, where my first thought in every situation was, how does this affect me? Humility means I am going to think of others first. This was a major culture shift for me, because I am innately selfish, we all are. We have to take on the mind of Christ. This scripture connects the dots between humility and love. You can't truly love without humility.

To have true humility in your life, we have to realize the enemy of humility is pride. There's that word again, pride. I am convinced that pride is the killer of most relationships. If we want to develop humility in our life, we must overcome pride and that takes work. It's nothing we can earn. We have to allow the Holy spirit to work in us and through us.

In Ephesians it says, *Be completely humble and gentle; be patient, bearing with one another in love.* [3] *Make every effort to keep the unity of the Spirit through the bond of peace.* If we want to keep unity in our marriages or any relationship, we must first be completely humble and eliminate pride from creeping through the cracks. This means, we may not get our way. Sometimes, to create peace, we need to keep our mouths closed. What happens after awhile, is that you will lose the desire to be right and you will also lose the desire to win. Your view of winning will be different than it used to be. Instead of winning the argument, which can't really be won anyway, you win their heart. Instead of being right all the time, the right thing to do is listen.

Everything begins and ends with humility. The message has a great spin on Proverbs 16, *"First pride, then the crash- the bigger the ego, the harder the fall."* I have first hand knowledge of this heartache. My pride got the best of me and the crash was devastating. I am thankful to say that I came out the other end, humbled, but if I don't work at it every day and remind myself of these truths, it could easily happen again. If you are filled with pride today, it's not too late to allow God to rid you of it. He will give you a new heart of humility that will change your world. This type of change will be evident to all of those around you. This type of change may require you to go through heartache. You may have to lose everything to gain the gift of humility. God's way of ridding you of pride, may be the most difficult process you go through, so make sure you are ready to allow God to rid of the very thing that can destroy you.

Repentance

Humility turns the light on our sin. It almost works as contact lenses into the soul, we can finally see our sin, our shame and where we went wrong. It allows us to finally understand our need to turn away from our sin and turn back to God. That's called repentance. It's like the old hymn that everyone knows, Amazing Grace, "I once was blind, but now I see."

Sometimes we need something traumatic to take place to draw close to God and allow Him to reopen our eyes. At times it's tragedy. Sometimes it's guilt or shame. It could simply be bad decisions, whatever the situation is that triggers the change. There is always a wake up call. One thing is for sure, sin always plays catch up and will find you no matter how hard you try to hide it.

If you don't believe me, ask David. Here we have a shepherd boy, who became a national hero and then a great warrior and then eventually a King. You would think that everything in his life was handed to him on a platter. He had it all, prestige, riches, good looks, strength, etc. Let's face it, he could have probably been a UFC champion in his day, if that was such a thing back in those days. I mean he did knock off one of the biggest giants in the land, Goliath. He was one bad (awesome) dude. No one wanted to mess with him. Surely a man like this wouldn't have any secret sins or issues that he struggled with? Of course, this couldn't be further from the truth.

One day David woke up from a nap and went for a stroll on the roof of the palace. That seems like an odd place for a stroll to me. Nevertheless, while on the roof, he had a perfect viewpoint to see a young lady taking a bath. Of course, David could have used the old trick of bouncing his eyes and moved on, but he didn't. He kept looking, obviously he was enamored by what he saw. So much so, that David asked about her and was told that she was Uriah's wife, Bathsheba. Even that bit of info didn't squelch his pursuit, he went after her with everything that he had.

He knew it was wrong, but lust had overtaken him. They ended up committing adultery and Bathsheba ended up pregnant. If David wasn't in enough hot water, this story takes a further downturn. He wanted to meet with Uriah and allow him to come home and be with his wife. The deception was conniving and sinful.

When sin permeates our heart, it has a snowball effect. Suddenly after awhile, it's an avalanche. Things were spinning out of control for David, but he didn't stop there. He would send a letter to Joab, telling him to put Uriah on the front lines, where the battle was the most fierce and make sure he was killed in battle. It was a despicable, vindictive act against one of his own men putting him in the hands of the enemy on purpose. Uriah would be killed on the battlefield. David's destructive plan was carried out. When Bathsheba heard of her husband's fate, she grieved deeply for Uriah. Then as the time of mourning was over, here comes David to conveniently pick up the pieces. They would end up getting married and would have a son. David's joy however, would quickly turn to agony as the son only lived a few days.

The Bible says that God was not pleased with what David had done and sent the prophet Nathan to him. Nathan shared a story with David that served as his wake up call. He told a story of a rich man and a poor man.

The rich man had many flocks of sheep and herds of cattle, adversely the poor man had one tiny female lamb. This little lamb grew up in this man's family.

It was like a daughter to him. One day the rich man had a dinner guest and he was too selfish to take one of his many riches of cattle or sheep, so he decided that he would take the poor man's tiny lamb. His one and only lamb, his pride and joy. After hearing this, David became angry. He said, whoever did this ought to be killed. He was appalled at the arrogance and selfishness of the rich man. David shouted that he should have to repay for what he did, multiple times over.

Nathan looks at David and says, "You're the man," he continues on, "and here's what God, the God of Israel, has to say to you: I made you king over Israel. I freed you from the fist of Saul. I gave you your master's daughter and other wives to have and to hold. I gave you both Israel and Judah. And if that hadn't been enough, I'd have gladly thrown in much more. So why have you treated the word of God with brazen contempt, doing this great evil? You murdered Uriah the Hittite, then took his wife as your wife. Worse, you killed him with an Ammonite sword! And now, because you treated God with such contempt and took Uriah the Hittite's wife as your wife, killing and murder will continually plague your family." This is God speaking, remember! "I'll make trouble for you out of your own family. I'll take your wives from right out in front of you. I'll give them to some neighbor, and he'll go to bed with them openly. You did your deed in secret; I'm doing mine with the whole country watching!"

After having his sin shown to him and hearing God's message through Nathan, David immediately confessed his sin. When the confession takes place, it begins the process of genuine repentance. At that very moment, David turned his heart back to God. Nathan proclaims that God forgave David's sin. What's interesting is that even though Nathan recounted David's long list of sins that happened over time, which I am sure was hard for David to listen to, God completely forgave David quickly. The litany of sins didn't matter.

God never holds grudges with us especially when we come to Him with our brokenness and a willingness to come back to Him. David's confession was honest and he took full responsibility for his actions. He never tried to put the blame on someone else. A true sign of authentic repentance is when you man up and take the blame. In the past, I would blame my wife for things that I did, I finally discovered that if I owned up to it, healing could then take place.

David also confessed his sin as sin. He didn't make any excuses or try to justify his sin. He called it exactly as it was. He was tired of running from his sin and trying to do it in secret. David was ready to expose his sin to God and truly become a man after God's own heart.

To become a man after God's heart, David needed to have a humble heart. This situation was certainly the genesis of this heart transplant that David so desperately needed. Unfortunately he had to go through immense pain to experience the transformation. Many times God uses those who go through that type of pain. He knows when his children lead from their brokenness, they can authentically present the message of hope and grace because they have experienced it themselves. God's grace is radical and his love is unconditional. When we experience that type of grace and love from Christ, we can easily share the same grace and love with others.

We serve a God that will forgive the darkest sins in our life and with the same breath love us with a love that is deeper than the deepest ocean. Grace is simply unmerited favor. We don't deserve it and can do nothing to earn it. In fact, if we received what we deserved, we would all receive death because that is the wages of our sin. It's simply out of His unconditional love for us that He chooses to extend grace to us. The goal is not to become perfect so then we can accept grace, it's in our imperfections that the grace of God shines through.

The Apostle Paul said that he asked God three times to take away the thorn in his side, his greatest weakness, but he said it brought him humility and drove him to his knees. Then God said, "My grace is sufficient for you, it's all you need. My power works best through your weakness." His grace is more than enough for each of us. Most of the time, our issue isn't if God's grace is sufficient, it's whether we will allow His grace to work in us. Will we accept His offer of grace or will we continue to dwell on our weaknesses.

For me, I was ready and willing to accept God's grace, I was desperate for it. I wanted to experience His strength, even through my imperfections. God offers His forgiveness and grace freely, don't wait until tomorrow to accept it. The sooner you accept grace in your heart, it will permeate your very being and you will experience a freedom that only God can give.

I am thankful that He knows me more than anyone in the world and still loves me. Even after the list of sins, He still loves me. He knows every struggle that I have or will have and still loves me. If David can be forgiven of his sins, we can to. You may be saying, my sins are worse or I have sinned more frequently than David. God isn't concerned about your past. He desires your heart, all of it. There isn't anything that we can do to make God love us more or less. He wants genuine repentance, the kind where He returns to the first place in your life. It may take pain and suffering, but God will use whatever it takes to draw people to him. He will surely use it for your good and His glory. Are you willing to go all the way and do what it takes?

I remember my parents telling me as a kid as they were punishing me, "We are doing this because we love you. This is for your own good." That was hard to understand as a child, because it wasn't fun to go through pain or suffering. We have to remember that God doesn't allow the crash to take place to hurt us or because He wants to watch us suffer. He does it because of the vast, unmeasurable love that He has for His children. He does it to draw us closer to Him and He gets the glory for the change.

CHAPTER 9
PAIN IS NEVER WASTED

I was finally experiencing freedom through God's grace and I was working through the process of restoration in my life, when the script was flipped even more.

Four months after my wife left, she made the difficult call and told me that that she wanted a divorce. It was the call I was dreading to hear and it became a reality.

I was completely floored. This wasn't the twist or turn that I was expecting. For me this came out of left field and I had a hard time understanding the decision. I kept telling myself that God was in control and that He had this in His hands, but even after processing this, I had a hard time connecting my heart to my head.

This news was more difficult to take than the original news of her leaving. At least then, I felt some type of hope. Now I was being told there was no hope. What do you do with that? Do you accept it and move on? That may sound like great advice, but when it's fresh, it's impossible for your heart to switch gears and turn on a dime. I don't know how people do that, I certainly couldn't. My heart wouldn't allow me to just automatically transition to the next season of life.

In a way, I felt like I was back to square one at the train station of Hopelessville, but after awhile of sulking when the tears had subsided, I came to the realization that God was still in the middle of this situation, even if the results weren't what I desired. I knew that God hadn't gone on vacation and wasn't leaving me behind in His dust. I had come too far over the last few months to give up. I knew that God wasn't done with me quite yet and I had so much to live for and fight for. I wasn't going to give up on my life just because it was dark or like the world told me to. God put a scripture on my heart that has been etched in my brain ever since. Galatians 6:9.

It says, *"So let's not get tired of doing what is good. At just the right time we will reap a harvest of blessing if we don't give up."*

God instructed me to keep planting seeds, because the harvest is coming, if I did't give up before it happened. I am not talking about the results of restoring my marriage, although I felt I did everything in my power to make that happen. I am talking about a greater blessing that God has in store for us, if we don't give up. Through our faithfulness to Him through hardship and trials, we reap rewards that can't be measured on this earth. It could mean that hearts may be won for Jesus or someone's life could be changed forever through my faithfulness and testimony. I had come to the place in my life that Jesus was more than sufficient in my life and He was my focus.

We can plant seeds that are negative or we can choose to plant seeds that are positive and uplifting. For too long I had been planting the wrong seeds, I was now planting the seeds that would produce a fruitful harvest.

What seeds are you planting in your life, seeds that will grow and flourish or seeds that will produce death and destruction? Rest assured, whatever you are planting it will harvest. I want to encourage you to plant the seeds that are filled with life and vitality, not seeds that destroy everyone and everything around you.

You may not be able to control your situation, it may be completely out of your hands, but one thing you can control is your response to the situation. This may be the most difficult season you will ever walk through in your entire life. You can choose to barricade yourself off from the rest of the world or you can scrape yourself off of the floor and carry on.

I will tell you there is no easy way out. There isn't a shortcut or detour that you can take to remove yourself from the process. This isn't Super Mario Brothers. You can't jump down into a tube and automatically be in a higher level. You can't fast forward this process because it's a refining process. At this point you may be in the middle of the storm, if you are not there currently. There is a good chance you will be one day. We all go through them and we all handle them differently. Whether it's an end to a dream or career, maybe it's a death of a loved one or maybe it's divorce. I know there are many who are going through a financial storm that feels like it will never go away. No matter the storm, you can't avoid it or go around it. You will have to go through.

The good news is that God goes with you through every storm. You can be assured of that. Whether you made decisions that perpetuated a storm or you were blindsided by it, you have a choice to make. Early on in the healing process, my counselor would tell me, you can choose to go through this storm or you can grow through this storm. I chose from the beginning to grow through it, allowing God to refine me through it and to change my heart, a change that would have never taken place without the storm. At some point in your life, you will begin to thank God for the storms that you have had to endure once you reach a different vantage point.

After I chose to grow through this trial, rather than go through it, I knew I wanted to be a different man on the other side of the storm than I was when I entered. It was a little bit like a car wash. Not the kind that you have to do yourself. I am talking about the type of car wash that lines up the tires on the tracks and takes you through the conveyer system automatically. If your car is like mine, it's filthy when it enters. Then it goes through an extensive process of not only washing the car, but it gets fully detailed. The wheels are washed, the tires are shined up and the car even gets dried at the end. You can absolutely get the works. Through this extensive process, when your car comes out of the other end, it's as if you have a new car. It doesn't look the same as it did when it went in.

The only problem is when we go through that process we forget the most important part, the part that we have to live with the most, the inside. We make the effort to get the outside looking pristine, but we live with the dust, dirt and last week's Bojangles lunch bag in the front seat. We think we are okay with the inside, as long as the outside looks spotless. However, the detailing of the car is only complete when the outside and the inside are completely overhauled.

Just like the car wash, the same is true with the storms in your life. You won't be the same again. If you choose to allow God to overhaul you through this process, drastic life change can and will take place. It will be an extensive process, it won't happen overnight but one thing is for sure, you will not be the same when you come out of the other side, but don't forget the most important part, the inside. Don't settle for the shiny exterior, while your heart rots from within. Make sure you get "the works" inside first and when you do, everything else changes from the inside out.

Your family and friends will see and experience the life change, you may even become unrecognizable to the people around you. The change that takes place in your heart will permeate your entire being and will rise to the surface for all to see.

God and God alone can make that change and He can use your storm to do it. Don't get frustrated with the process. It is the very thing that may drive you to be the person that God calls you to be.

Rick Warren said, "There is purpose in the pain." I believe that God uses every drop of pain as fuel to drive you to become the person He desires you to be. It's never wasted and never useless. There is great meaning in every ounce. He uses it to shape people and build maturity in their faith. I honestly believe that God is using the pain that I have felt and has made me a stronger person because of it, even the pain that was caused by my own actions and decisions. We all need to experience some type of pain in our life to slow us down and to stir us to a greater faith in Christ.

Metamorphosis

The word "metamorphosis" derives from the Greek, meaning "transformation, transforming," "change" or "to form."

"We delight in the beauty of the butterfly, but rarely admit the changes it has gone through to achieve that beauty." Maya Angelou

I love this quote from Maya Angelou. I remember going to the Tennessee Aquarium with Tiffany and the kids when they were young. Along the tour we entered into this beautiful butterfly garden. These unique, small but lively creatures were so incredible. They were filled with life and radiated such a vibrant color. But they weren't always that way. The humble beginnings include larvae and then a caterpillar that crawls and then they morph or transform into a gorgeous flying creature. A creature that kids and adults alike, marvel every time one would fly close enough to us.

Our Christian journey is so much like this metamorphosis. It is a process of refining that takes time, it certainly doesn't happen automatically. When we enter into a season of growth, we begin by removing all of the old chains of self and our past and we put on a new robe of righteousness. Then we offer ourselves as a living sacrifice, a piece of moldable clay for God to create whatever He desires for our life. That is the part of submission or surrender that we all must do and thankfully He does the morphing/transforming into a Christ-like image.

Our process is never completed. However, the moment we feel like we have achieved transformation is the moment that God changes us again and begins a new process of refining. We have a tendency to try to wiggle out of the cocoon before we are ready to come out.

I heard Pastor Greg Rohlinger talk about this in his sermon a while back. Greg was diagnosed with a rare disease and was given only a few years to live, so he knew all about the refining process. He said, "*If you want to short circuit what God is doing, open the cocoon. When you open the cocoon, you will find a butterfly that's not ready.*" He went on to say, "*It's in the struggling of fighting out of the cocoon, where the butterfly finds its wings and they find strength.*" If you are going through a struggle right now, don't fight it. He is preparing your strength for what He is already preparing for you! He's not giving up on you! Don't give up on the process.

Transformation is possible and likely with God if we are willing to submit to His refining. He can turn the ugliest piece of dirt, a part that has been lost in the ashes and transform them into the most beautiful creature known to man. The cool part of this process is that the means of which this is possible took place at the cross. He sent His Son and that was the conduit for change in us. It is not about what things we do or what processes we create to be a better person. It's not about us at all, it's all about Him. Our part of this process is to simply say, change me and He who started the work in us is certainly faithful to complete the change!

Every morning I wake up with the need to be more obedient and more willing to be a living sacrifice and allow Him to mold me. I have learned how to appreciate the refining process, rather than reject it. We have to remember that we are the clay and He is the sculptor. The clay never tells the sculptor what to create. The clays only responsibility is to have an active willingness to be obedient and also have the patience to endure the process. For me, the process was just now beginning.

CHAPTER 10
THE PROCESS

Over the next few weeks and months, I became intimately acquainted with the promises of God. My relationship with Christ was strengthening to a place that it had never been before. Through my time in the Word, I began to explore the Old Testament book of Nehemiah. I felt drawn by the Holy Spirit to begin to study this book thoroughly. I knew the story in detail but I felt it never applied to me before, at least not until now. I suppose I forgot that all of God's word is applicable and alive with knowledge and hope. I began to read this story and I knew immediately that God was speaking to me through His Word.

Nehemiah was an ordinary man who was a cupbearer. The cupbearer in those days was a high ranking servant position, but it was still a servant position. A cupbearer was in charge of protecting the king from potential assassination through poisoning and would have to taste the wine before serving the king. It was an honor to be trustworthy enough to serve as cupbearer. God used this cupbearer to do great things in his homeland in ways no one ever imagined.

Throughout scripture God used ordinary people just like Nehemiah to do extraordinary tasks. This is why we should never think we are too ordinary or not equipped enough to complete the task that God is calling us to.

Just to set the stage, Jerusalem had been in ruins for 100 years. This city was filled with nothing but rubble. One day, God called Nehemiah to go back to rebuild the wall. Keep in mind, Nehemiah wasn't an architect and had no experience in construction. His qualifications didn't matter to God, he was the right man for the job. Nehemiah accepted the calling and began the process. Through Nehemiah's obedience, he took on the enormous task that everyone thought was impossible, rebuilding the wall of Jerusalem. Once again God showed that the word impossible had little meaning to Him.

I heard Christine Caine say recently in a message, *"Impossible is where God starts. God turns up when everything else is exhausted, that's when you are poised for a miracle!"*

For 100 years nothing had changed, the city was still filled with rubble. God sought someone who was going to rise up and stand by God's Word, no matter what others thought. He wasn't looking for the most dynamic leader with a tremendous amount of experience. He called someone who was obedient and a person who would never give up, even when signs pointed that he should. God was bigger than the challenge that Nehemiah faced and he continued to persevere, even when the world didn't understand.

Through the Holy Spirit, Nehemiah was able to conquer the enemy and finish the work that God called him to do. Nehemiah went to Jerusalem and just 52 days later, the wall was completed! I believe that with the Holy Spirit and your obedience, you can see victory in your life. You can see the breakthrough that you have been praying about for so long.

In this chapter, we are going to explore the process that Nehemiah went through to complete this supernatural task. It is the blueprint that I used in my own life to draw closer to God and to see a full heart transformation through His spirit.

First and foremost, you need to ask yourself what are the ashes or the rubble in my life? For the Jewish people they were settling for the rubble, God wanted to do so much more for them, but they were okay with living in the ashes. At some point in our lives, we have to not be okay with the ashes and we need to have a desire for more.

We fall into a rut in life and we can't get out of it. For some people it's addiction, it may be struggles in your marriage, or it may be the pain of losing a loved one. Whatever it is, life is too brief to settle for less than what God desires for you. He desires your faithfulness and obedience. It is a simple concept but it takes more than just willingness, it takes action and commitment.

The first thing that you have to buy into is the belief that God wants something greater for you. Don't settle for going through the motions and doing enough to be a "good Christian." The greater that He has for you isn't vast riches of earthly treasures, but a peace that comes with knowing that you are completely in the center of God's will. If you believe that there is more to this life than the routine, then you have to be willing to fight for it. I didn't realize I needed to fight for my marriage until after it was nearly over. You don't have to wait until the end to begin to fight and rebuild what has been destroyed. You can choose today to rebuild and gain victory again. Nehemiah decides to rebuild, gathered the people and completed the task. He doesn't talk about it for 10 years and then develop a plan for 10 more, he just did it! The decision to do it is the easy part. Just because you decide to do it, doesn't mean that it won't take work, patience and determination. The process begins by evaluating your current situation.

Evaluate the Damage

I slipped out during the night, taking only a few others with me. I had not told anyone about the plans God had put in my heart for Jerusalem. We took no pack animals with us except the donkey I was riding. After dark I went out through the Valley Gate, past the Jackal's Well, and over to the Dung Gate to inspect the broken walls and burned gates. Then I went to the Fountain Gate and to the King's Pool, but my donkey couldn't get through the rubble. So, though it was still dark, I went up the Kidron Valley instead, inspecting the wall before I turned back and entered again at the Valley Gate. Nehemiah 2:12-15

Before Nehemiah put one hammer to a nail, he went out in the middle of the night to check out the damage. He wanted to see what he was up against. He also wanted to develop a plan to get the job done. After my divorce, I went into self-evaluation mode. I wanted God to search me and know my heart. My desire was to be shaped by Him and for everything that I was doing to be pleasing to Him. I asked God to take away the things in my life that needed to be eliminated and add the things that needed to be added. To do this, you have to be honest and real with yourself. It's also good to ask others who are consistently around you and let them evaluate you. Don't be afraid to have your feelings hurt, their response may be unkind to your ears, but it may be exactly what you need. This is another reason why accountability and counseling are crucial to the process.

I made a list of things I wanted to change in my life and ways that God can change me. It wasn't a matter if God would change me it was only a matter of me giving God the room to do so. We have to give God room to move in the situation. He can't work if you always have your hands in it and there is no room for His hands. God wants to change things in your life, but you have to be willing to let go of your desires and let go of the control.

Nehemiah could have gone out and inspected the walls and come back with the conclusion that many of us do, "This is beyond repair." He could have easily told himself, "There is just way too much rubble, I will never see this rebuilt." Those thoughts are from the enemy. The enemy wants you to believe that there is too much damage or the ashes are too many. The enemy will do anything in his power to convince you that it's impossible.

You may be looking at your marriage and saying, there is too much pain, too much hurt to carry on. You may try to convince yourself that it would be easier for everyone involved if you just gave up. You may think about your addiction and say to yourself, why bother, there is too much damage to turn this around. This looks too broken to put it back together again, it may be humanly impossible. That's the problem, with you doing it on your own, it is impossible and more than likely it will never happen.

However here's the good news, with God, impossible is not a valid word. The rubble is never too great, the pain never too insurmountable that God cannot heal. Even if you have given up and said, it's not worth it, you can still come back from that. Don't let pride prevent you from being where you need to be. Pick up the shovel and clean the rubble, then pick up the hammer and lay one brick at a time. Piece by piece, brick by brick, God will give you the strength to rebuild the destruction in your life.

The greatest miracles in the Bible happened after all human hope was gone. In John 11, Lazarus was in the tomb for four days, the people thought his spirit had left his body. Jesus didn't come to heal him, because some things need to die in our life before they can be revived. God was clearly strategic in wanting everyone to lose hope to show how powerful He really is. Lazarus was dead and gone but God had other plans. He still moved and Lazarus lived!

Whatever is dead in your life, even if you have lost all hope, remember God can resurrect it from the ashes even after you thought it was dead. If you feel further away from God than you ever have, it's never too late to have your relationship with Christ revived. Call on Him and He will answer, He will come right where you are and pick you up with His loving arms and take you back.

People Will Call You Crazy!

"Becoming obsessed with what people think is the quickest way to forget about what God thinks." Craig Groeschel

Remember this process of rebuilding and restoration won't be easy. It takes work and there may be some growing pains that you will have to work through. People around you may not understand. In fact some will call you crazy for not giving up.

The world that we live in today is quick to judge and quick to give up and at times we are surrounded with negativity due to other people's past hurts. During times of struggle it's best to surround yourself with people who are going to encourage you, but we always need to make sure the encouragement comes through the lens of scripture. I heard Leonard Sweet say that it's God's responsibility to judge, it's the Holy Spirit's responsibility to convict and it's our responsibility to love. The critics in your life who won't understand your stance will not have the point of view that God gives you.

Nehemiah continued to be obedient, never gave up and that turned out pretty well for him! He was faithful to his calling and obedient to the Father. In my life, I want to be foolish like Nehemiah! I want to be crazy, crazy obedient that is.

All of us have a little absurdity in our makeup. I believe we can channel that absurdity for good. Let's face it, not many people who were called to do something audacious in scripture were without critics or opposition. That comes with the territory of following God. If we were more concerned about what God says rather than others, we would be able to do so much for Christ. What is God calling you to do that might make others cringe or question? If it doesn't have that type of response, then maybe your dream isn't audacious enough.

Whatever God has called you to conquer in your life, rest assured, He gives you the right tools to complete it. He did it with Nehemiah and He will do it with you.

Extreme, Radical Obedience

"A man named Jesus made a paste and rubbed it on my eyes and told me, 'Go to Siloam and wash.' I did what he said. When I washed, I saw." John 9

This sounds crazy! But this teaches us a simple principle. Do what He says and you can't go wrong! The blind man was explaining the miracle and the only explanation was Jesus said to do it and he did it and it happened, even though it doesn't make any sense to rub wet dirt or sand in someone's eyes. Usually that is the very thing that makes you not be able to see.

Even though it didn't make sense and people couldn't understand it and I am sure there were naysayers but that didn't matter to him. He did it and it happened. His faith and radical obedience made him well. He was at a place of desperation and he knew that it required extreme faith and extreme measures to see his miracle.

The first leap of faith was his willingness to let Jesus touch his eyes with spit and mud. I would probably think that you had lost your mind if you touched my eyes with that. The second leap of faith was to go to the pool of Siloam and wash it out. There were no guarantees it was going to work. There was no assurance of anything. He just had faith, he didn't need to see progress or be encouraged that it was the right thing to do. It was between Him and Jesus. He believed, he obeyed and he saw.

It's such a short scripture with so much depth and stories to learn from. So no matter if others think it's impossible or that you are crazy, remain faithful and obedient to God, because your miracle is coming. It may take you going through the spit and sand in your eyes. It may take going through the sludge and pain of this life but through those storms God is preparing us for our miracle.

However, the miracle that you may be seeking may not be the one that God has for you. This is a story that's really not about the result. It's about a blind man's obedience to Christ. God did bless his obedience by healing him, but sometimes God's greatest blessings are found in the healing that doesn't take place, the marriage that isn't restored and the sick loved one who doesn't make it through the cancer. I know this is a hard pill to swallow, but the blessing may be found in ways that we could have never imagined.

God help us to be like the blind man and stand strong and show radical obedience and extreme faith in a God that heals and restores, even in ways that we don't understand.

Sometimes we have to go through the mud, spit and dirtiness of life to get to the good stuff, we get to the point where we get so fed up with failure and disappointment that we are willing to do anything to follow Christ and His way!

Nehemiah had to walk through the days of rubble, before the wall was rebuilt. Even before he laid one brick, there were people telling him, it's impossible. These people were discouragers, naysayers and the doubters. I'm sure you have these people in your life. No matter what you try to do, they think you can't do it or it's impossible. They have told you that you are not equipped, you are not smart enough, or that you will never accomplish what you set out to do.

It never fails, someone will also try to stand in our way and give us the wrong advice because it is what they believe, not what the Word says. We need to recognize this for what it really is. It's an attack from the enemy. Anytime we take a leap of faith for Christ, the enemy will attack. How are you responding to the enemy when these attacks begin to fly?

In the book of Nehemiah it says, *We must guard our hearts, day and night.* (Nehemiah 4:9, NIV) A few verses later he gives us a strategy to defend. *We must post our defenses in our weakest points, ready to defend, with other followers, with the strength of His word, with the power of the Holy Spirit.* (Nehemiah 4:13, NIV)

There is a point where Nehemiah instructs his crew to keep building with one hand and fighting with a sword in the other fending off the enemy. What would happen if we woke up every day with that mindset? If you are like me, I double check to make sure I have everything that I need before I leave for the day. My car keys- check, my wallet- check and I certainly couldn't forget my cell phone. That would be a travesty. What if we were to walk out the door every morning with the two things that we really needed the most to face the day, a sword and a hammer. A hammer to continue to build the very thing that has called you to build in your life and a sword to protect that calling from the enemy. I believe we could become warriors for the Gospel if we carried those two very crucial tools. Many times, we will carry one without the other. We will pick up the hammer and literally hammer away at what God has called us to do. We tend to forget that the enemy doesn't want that to happen and certainly doesn't want us to be fruitful. All of our hammering goes by the wayside, because it doesn't last, spiritual warfare is too strong to overcome. The same can be true when you just have the sword. You are fighting off the enemy but fail to be productive. The enemy uses the weapon of distraction and gets you off of the course that God has set forth. That is why we need both the hammer and the sword.

If you really think about the distractions and the opposition that they faced and they still built the wall in 52 days. This is nothing short of a miracle, which is just another day for our God.

CHAPTER 11

52 DAY JOURNEY

As I began to read the book of Nehemiah about a man that had a tremendous journey, I felt God leading me to begin a new journey of growth myself. I was inspired by the faith and obedience of Nehemiah in the midst of a dire, seemingly impossible, situation. I felt, in many ways, that I was in the same spot of desperation that Nehemiah found himself in.

For the people of Jerusalem, they were stuck, mired in the ashes of the wall. They had settled for that being their destiny and outcome, but Nehemiah saw so much more in the midst of the ashes. He saw potential and felt the calling by God to change it. Remember the walls lay in ruins for 100 years. Nehemiah could have very easily said, this is the way it is and it will never change, but no, he knew with God, anything is possible and change can happen.

God wasn't leading me to build a wall, but he certainly wanted to rebuild something in me and I had to allow Him to do something special within my heart that would change my course and set forth a season of tremendous growth. I felt led to go on a 52 day journey of prayer, fasting and devotion to God. This season proved to be the most significant spiritual season of growth in my entire life.

In order to have the willingness for change, you must first surrender everything, not just 98 or 99%. You have to give all of yourself to Christ. Rick Warren says that the pathway to peace is surrender. You must relinquish all of your rights and all of the control you think you have. We must submit all of our hopes and dreams to Christ. It's funny, I used to equate submission with giving up and losing, but now I know that real submission to God is the only way to achieve complete victory and find true peace within Christ. I was desperate to see victory and I wanted to truly see change in my life.

Before I entered into this 52 day journey, I had to hand everything over to Christ, this included the very thing I couldn't change, my marital status. As much as I wanted to try to hold on to Tiffany, I knew I had to let go and submit my family and future to Him. This didn't mean I would stop caring or loving my family, it also doesn't mean I lost hope that God could still do a miracle. It's quite the opposite. There is a major difference between giving up and letting go. I understood that surrender was the key to slaying the dragons in my life. It's when we hand the sword over to the Father and watch Him fight the enemy! Whatever your dragon is today, remember that God is fighting for you, so don't give up, rest in Him and let Him fight the battle. The battle belongs to the Lord, not you.

It was a difficult lesson to learn but completely necessary for me. There is such a freedom that comes through surrender. Everyone needs a white flag moment in their life where you give your broken ruins over to God and let Him turn what was meant for evil into something good. The time we spend dealing with our junk on our own is wasted time that we should be busy submitting it to God and resting in His goodness. When we try to run to ourselves to fix us or the problem, we end up running in circles because we are right there.

We get drained of everything good in our lives because it's not satisfying. We tend to create further disaster and our lives become an even bigger mess! If only we would run to Him and allow Him to carry us through our mess, rather than trying to run our own show.

Steven Furtick said, *"The only way for God to show me that He's in control is to put me in a situation that's outside of my control. It may be out of the realm of my control but it's not out of the realm of God's capability and power."* Surrender means I can trust God to fight the battle, because it's not mine to fight anyway, it's His. Turn it over and let Him work!

Once surrender took place, I began to reinstall spiritual disciplines in my life that I let fall by the wayside. If you want to see God move in your life, draw closer to Him by being around everything that He's involved in. These were the keys to my 52 day journey with Christ. These are the very components that could change your course.

1. Prayer Life Revitalized

My prayer life was changed not only because I was intentional about it, but also because I changed the way I prayed. For so long I had been praying in a selfish way. I was trying to evoke God's power to correspond with my plans. I learned during this journey that if I really wanted to see change, I would need to pray God's will to be activated to support His plan for my life. This wasn't simply carving out a certain time of day where I would communicate with God. It was a constant flow of communication with Him. If you want to build or rebuild your relationship with Christ, you begin by spending time with Him.

I remember when I first fell in love with Tiffany, I didn't want to leave her side. I wanted to be around her 24/7 because I wanted our relationship to grow and the only way to do that was to spend quality time with each other. That is what God desires from you, He wants your time and attention. It's in those moments that you are committing everything to Him, that's when you begin to see Him pour into your life again. He sees the investment and appreciates your willingness to draw close to Him.

James 4:8 says *Come close to God, and God will come close to you. Wash your hands, you sinners; purify your hearts, for your loyalty is divided between God and the world.*

The more steps you take toward Him, the more He will take toward you. When this happens, His presence is much more palpable in your life. Throughout this season of growth, I was focused daily on Him and lost focus of the chaos of my life. I noticed that when you are in the presence of God, the chaos begins to fade away and we receive so much peace and joy.

2. Hunger for the Word

I began several reading plans from the YouVersion app. One of those plans was called 30 in 30. I read through the entire New Testament in 30 days. I can't tell you the impact this had on my life. During this 52 day journey, something happened in my heart in regards to God's Word. God instilled in me once again the passion and hunger for the word, much like a hunger for food. I began to wake up every morning and crave God's word, as if I needed it to survive.

We all need the Word of God to survive. Jesus said it explicitly: Man doesn't live by bread alone but by every Word that comes from the mouth of God.

That became my desire. He began to open up my eyes to certain passages of scripture, my senses were heightened and I began to hear scripture in new ways.

In Nehemiah 8:8 it says, *They read from the Book of the Law of God and clearly explained the meaning of what was being read, helping the people understand each passage.*

A few verses later it says, they celebrated because they finally understood what they were reading. Something happened, a switch was flipped and God gave great clarity and understanding. That is exactly what I felt as I began to read the word of God in a new light.

3. Fasting

We should fast when we desire to draw closer to God. Fasting is not just a discipline for bringing problems to God to be fixed. It is also an expression of the heart's longing for a greater intimacy in our walk with Him. It is to set aside our physical appetites in order to focus more of our time and attention upon the Lord.

Fasting is an exciting venture because it focuses us upon a deeper relationship with God. **God is a jealous God who gives Himself most fully to those who give themselves to Him most completely.** The discipline of fasting helps us to give ourselves more fully to the Lord by putting the ax to any tendencies we have that would distract our focus from Him. It develops in us a consistency of devotion that draws us into God's confidence in which He is pleased to walk with us and talk with us.

There is something supernatural that takes place when God's people fast and pray. I have noticed that in my life every time that I have felt led to do so. Fasting brings alignment and alignment is always necessary to stay on course. Take your car, for instance, when it gets out of alignment, it will veer off its course and crash on the side of the road if it's bad enough.

The same thing happens in our life, if we don't stay in perfect alignment with God's purposes and His will, then we will veer off course and crash and burn. That is what happened to me. Fasting is the very component that gets you realigned with God's will and prevents you from the crash and burn.

You don't have to fast from food, there could be many things that you fast. I do believe that fasting from food is important because it's the one necessity that we have a natural hunger for.

During this intense time of prayer and fasting, God gave me a new vision and passion for my life found in Him, not in my circumstances or other people. I was satisfied solely by Christ and He opened up my senses to worship Him more fully and completely.

4. Accountability Support

Another component was to reinstall accountability measures back into place and build a prayer support system. I assembled a team of over 80 people to pray for me during the 52 day journey. I could feel their support and encouragement every single day. The outpouring of love and grace was simply incredible. I also assembled a group of 6 men to be on my personal board of directors. These men were trusted and had permission to tell me exactly how they felt. If they saw something in me that wasn't pleasing, I wanted them to voice their concerns. This is something I wish I had assembled long before the crash.

It's never too late to put people in your life who lift you up, be honest with you and encourage you. The bottom line is, you can't do this on your own. You need as many people who will support you as possible.

Two are better than one, because they have a good reward for their toil. For if they fall, one will lift up his fellow. But woe to him who is alone when he falls and has not another to lift him up! Again, if two lie together, they keep warm, but how can one keep warm alone? And though a man might prevail against one who is alone, two will withstand him — a threefold cord is not quickly broken. Ecclesiastes 4:9-12

5. Sing Through the Storm

Acts 16:25 says, *About midnight Paul and Silas were praying and singing hymns to God, and the prisoners were listening to them.*

Keep in mind, Paul and Silas were in prison, probably living through a rough season. All they could do was sing of God's faithfulness and pray. I have noticed that as my journey progressed throughout this year of growth, I began to worship God more and more, celebrating God's faithfulness. Even though my circumstances were dark, He was still good and worthy to be praised. Lyrics of songs began to come to life for me. My prayer life went to a new level.

My relationship with Christ was strengthening. I want to encourage you to sing, even when it hurts, just shout to the Heavens. Even when you begin to doubt what you are singing, sing anyway. In those moments, God does something genuine in your life and you begin to believe and it becomes real to you again. Even when the walls are shaking, keep singing, your breakthrough is coming!

6. Serve Through the Heartache

A while back I was walking in downtown Orlando, when I met a young man named Anthony. It was very crowded in the area that I saw Anthony in and he approached me and I struck up a conversation. My first question was where are you from? He said that he was from Washington, DC and had come to be in a warmer climate. His wife had left him, emptied his bank account and took everything including the blinds off the windows. I told him that I could relate to the fact that his wife left him but then I thought, I can't really relate to him at all. He was living on the streets. He didn't even have a pillow to lay his head on each night. I was so caught up in my own mess that I was completely oblivious to the rest of the world. Sometimes we have to get out of our bubble and invest in others to realize that our world is really, really small and insignificant!

By stepping out of my own shadow on that evening it taught me that loving others takes the focus off of my own situation and draws me even closer to Christ. That night I discovered that serving others through my own heartache advances the healing of my heart, not to mention the impact that we can have on others.

Anthony never asked for anything on that night with the exception of prayer. He knew that I was a pastor and he said that he wanted to be blessed, little did he know on that night I was more blessed by him than he was by me.

If you want to stop thinking about your issues or your pain, focus on someone else's and help them along the journey. Whether it's lending a listening ear, physical labor or even a genuine smile, you will be amazed how the healing works both ways.

The Midway Point

Before Nehemiah and his team reached their breakthrough of rebuilding the wall, which was a task that everyone said couldn't be done, there were several tests involved. The enemy tried everything in his power to derail the supernatural, but we all know that never works. Something took place around the midway point of the wall construction, the faithful workers hit the old proverbial wall while ironically, building a wall.

Nehemiah 4:6 says, *So we rebuilt the wall till all of it reached half its height, for the people worked with all their heart.*

They had absolutely given everything to this project, blood, sweat and probably some tears. They were also emotionally spent, because of the enemy's attack. Sanballat and his gang of misfits continued to do everything they could to halt their progress. Not only were they emotionally and physically drained, they were completely discouraged by their progress.

Meanwhile, the people in Judah said, "The strength of the laborers is giving out, and there is so much rubble that we cannot rebuild the wall."

They honestly felt like packing it in and taking it to the house. Have you ever felt like you were knocking it out of the park, giving every bit of yourself and then not see any results?

Several years ago, I remember putting together a gas grill without any directions. I wasn't challenging myself to see if I could do it, the manufacturer left them out of the box. It felt like I was working on that thing for hours and I just didn't see the progress, even after the time and sweat.

I believe the enemy knows that at the midway point, before you get over the hump, is the greatest opportunity for discouragement and an all out attack. The excitement and the momentum are gone and there seems to be so many reasons to just quit.

I got to the halfway point of my journey and I felt this same wave of discouragement. The newness had worn off and I felt like I wasn't making any progress, in fact I felt I had gone in the opposite direction with Tiffany. Then I remembered, I wasn't doing it for immediate gratification or to change the outcome, I was doing it so God could change me.

I could certainly relate with the Jewish people, I knew I had been working hard, but there was so much more rubble to clear out. I was still standing in the ashes and didn't see a way out. I discovered that at times it's counterproductive to measure progress. How do we measure it anyway? When the future is unclear, God isn't asking for a checklist or a completion chart, He simply wants us to keep our head down, put one foot in front of the other and keep moving. Keep fighting by picking up the hammer with one hand getting the task done and keep the sword in the other, fending off the enemy, the enemy that is trying to derail your progress.

This is how the workers changed their heart. Nehemiah simply said, *"Don't be afraid of them. Remember the Lord, who is great and awesome, and fight for your families, your sons and your daughters, your wives and your homes."* You may be standing at the crossroads and you are discouraged and frustrated. There are some of you, who are married right now but you are thinking about leaving. Some of you may have already left and you see no hope for your marriage. You are tired and you look down at your feet and you are knee deep in ashes. You don't foresee a way that these ashes could go away.

I want to encourage you that this is the midway point and this is the same spiritual warfare that Nehemiah and his friends were facing. I want to remind you that our God is great and awesome and He is calling you to fight for your family, your sons and daughters, your wives or husbands, and your homes. Despite what you feel, they are worth fighting for! It may require more hard work and perseverance, more sweat and maybe even more tears, but I can assure you it's worth it. Don't give up, keep fighting and refuse to go down!

At this point, I could have very easily given up my pursuit for God's will in my life. I could have given up on my desire to ever be used by God again, but He wouldn't let me quit. I knew that God had birthed in me a desire to live for Him and serve Him for the rest of my life and I knew that He had a greater role for me to play in building His Kingdom.

After 52 days, the walls were miraculously completed. What the opposition said couldn't be done, had been conquered. It was one of the most unlikely victories in history and it happened because they refused to quit.

The Bible says at the end of the 52 days, the enemy was afraid and fled. I would have loved to have been a fly on the wall to see that. God was with them, every step of the way, even when it felt like He wasn't. Not only was God present for those 52 days, He worked through them in ways no one thought was even possible. He used an ill-equipped, unprofessional, unskilled man to lead a revolution and they achieved victory. This is a prime example of God taking ashes and creating something beautiful out of it.

When we are willing to fight and are obedient, He can take whatever has burned down in our lives and restore it. He is the God of restoration. His specialty is to breathe life into dead things. The Jewish people experienced death when their city was destroyed and God showed them that He has the final word. He can bring your marriage out of the ashes and breathe new life into it. Even after divorce, He can resurrect it. I have seen it so many times and I have heard so many stories of God's faithfulness to breathe life into what once was seemingly dead.

Isaac and Denisha were married for 10 years, had a wonderful ministry, but circumstances led to a heartbreaking divorce in 2003. They didn't see a way out and they felt their marriage had become hopeless, so they decided on divorce and end everything. After the divorce, God began to work on their hearts and change them as individuals. 6 years later, yes 6 years later, God restored their marriage and their family! They were remarried in 2009 and now God is blessing them in ways that they never thought were possible.

I tell you this story to give you hope but be cautious to compare your situation to others. Every situation is different and we can fall into a comparison trap and that is a dangerous place. I admit there have been many times that I have read countless stories and seen literally hundreds of video testimonies of restoration. While hearing these stories, I would think, "If God can do that in their marriage or in their lives, why can't He do it for me?" The answer is simple, He can, but it won't be the same as others. Just because He can doesn't mean He will. There may something greater that He wants to teach you through this situation. There are different factors and different circumstances that make the healing process varied. There isn't a formula for restoration other than surrender and obedience. Even then, the question of when can't be answered. His timing needs to be trusted, so be careful to compare your story to others. It can leave you disappointed when it doesn't turn out the way and in the amount of time you witness in other cases. God has a plan for you.

At the end of the 52 day journey, the Jewish people had been united and were extremely thankful for what God had done. At the end of my 52 day journey I sensed that same unity with Christ. My relationship with Him was as strong as ever. I wasn't a completed product nor did I have it all figured out, but I was a work in progress and I was finally being obedient to Christ every single day.

Thankfully God never stops His rebuilding project in us. The journey never stops. There should be constant movement in your relationship with Him at all times. We should mirror our relationship with others with that same blueprint in mind. We should never be stagnant. We should continue the perpetual motion to keep the relationship strong and healthy. Through His strength and our obedience we can see anything rebuilt in our lives.

I want to warn you though, if you choose to go on your own 52 day journey, don't expect magic to happen in 52 days. There is nothing magical within the number 52. I believe we should always expect miracles to take place, but this can be the preparation ground for God to do a mighty work in your life. This will be the catalyst for spiritual growth that will launch you to greater things in the future. He can still provide that miracle, but it will happen within His time frame.

He is the same God that can count the number of stars in the sky because He placed them there. He is God and if He created the planet, don't you think He can save your marriage. He is the God that fed 5,000 men with some fish and bread and still had leftovers to give out doggy bags. Don't you think He can provide for you in your time of financial need? He is also the God that healed a woman who had been suffering for over a decade, just by her merely touching His robe. If He did that, surely He can heal you of your physical and emotional ailments. He did, He can and He will! It may not happen on this side of eternity, as we will discover in the next chapter, but God's perfect will is always done. No matter the results, God is still God and He is still good. There is always hope found in Him.

CHAPTER 12
DIVINE INTERRUPTIONS

In August of 2011, one month before the official launch of the church plant, I received a call that no one wants to get. It was my sister and she was hysterical. She just simply said, "He's gone, Dad is gone!" I didn't want to believe it. I felt so helpless being so far away. I told my sister to go back in and make sure that he's really gone but there was no use, it was real. At the age of 50 my father had passed into eternity with His Heavenly Father. He wasn't feeling well that day and my mom went to grab something to eat and when she came back, he was face down on the bedroom floor and he was gone. He had a massive heart attack caused by heart disease and God took him home to heaven.

As soon as I heard the news, my knees buckled and I began to cry out to God. I had never cried so hard in my life. Maybe it was because it was so unexpected, maybe because I had never lost anyone in my life that was so close to me. The news was completely devastating to me and I remember being on the floor crying and pleading with God for this not to be my reality. I didn't want to believe the devastating news. I was immediately overcome with grief and utter emptiness, a feeling that I had never felt in my life.

I never imagined that I would have to tell my kids that night that their Grand-dude was gone. Yes, that's what they called him. In a matter of hours we would hop on a plane and head to Chattanooga to take care of the arrangements. As soon as we landed, I felt I had to play the role of taking the load. My mother and sister were obviously destroyed and I had to be strong for them and the rest of my family.

Reflecting back, I never had the opportunity or time to grieve as a son because I was too busy helping others go through the grieving process. I wrote the obituary, preached part of the funeral and tried to be strong. I helped pick out a casket and the music. I was involved with all of the details that go into a funeral. I'm certainly not using this as an excuse to be spiritually drained, but I certainly think this traumatic experience contributed to the emptiness inside of me. Hundreds of people came to the visitation and the funeral service was standing room only. It was a beautiful day to honor my father and ultimately it honored God, our Heavenly Father in such a special way.

Anytime someone dies at 50, there will always be questions, words left unsaid and moments left undone. In all fairness, I did question God when it happened. I believe it's only natural to feel that way. I told God that I had plans to spend more time with my dad. There was a bucket list that I wanted to accomplish with him. I wanted to see my dad get old and for him to watch my kids grow up. I could have easily lived with regrets but I chose to be thankful for the moments I had with my dad and refused to become bitter about the years I missed with him.

Earlier in the book I described the dissension with my dad. To say we had a tumultuous relationship for the first 20 plus years of my life would be an understatement, but that is only part of the story. The last few years of his life reminded us that people can change, truly change. In fact, he showed us that it's never too late to change and it proved that any relationship can be mended by God. My dad went from being my Kryptonite to being the dad I always desired. Even though his life was cut short, I was able to experience some tremendous moments with him, moments that will always be in my heart.

My dad was an original. In a world of parody, his type was rare. He was one of a kind, No one was like my dad. He was far from perfect, but let me give you a newsflash, neither am I and this may come as a surprise to some of you, but neither are you. Through his imperfections Stewart Johnson would be transformed by God into a very special and caring father.

A few years ago, my family went back to Chattanooga to celebrate Christmas. It was so good to be home and ever since my kids were born, my relationship with my father was very special. We were out in his garage and he was working on a car, because he truly had a passion and a gift when it came to body work and painting cars. He loved it and he was so good at it. He was showing me a piece of sheet metal and I tried to seem interested, I never received the passion for cars like he did. But I just wanted to spend time with him. I yearned for that especially after not receiving that growing up. As he was showing me the piece of metal, I reached out my hand and I accidentally sliced my hand open on the sheet metal. Dad immediately dropped the piece of metal and very gently took me by the hand.

Keep in mind, I was 26 years old at the time. He took me inside and went straight to the sink in the kitchen. He carefully washed the water over my wound and bandaged it up. It was almost as if he making up for lost time and I truly believe it symbolically cleansed and mended our relationship. The past didn't matter, just like Jesus wipes away our past, He throws our past as far as the east is from the west. My relationship with my father was based on that same grace and mercy. The last 10 years of his life we got so close, I can't remember an ill word that we said to each other during that time.

I could hear the pride in his voice when he talked to me and always asked about my church that I was planting and he was always looking for ways to help. He called me a couple of months before he passed away and told me that he was going to start mowing some of the neighbor yards so he could give the money to the church. He was selfless because he discovered that this world's treasures weren't important. Having a relationship with God was the most important thing.

Several years ago, my dad was visiting my house and it was late at night. Dad was struggling with life as all of us have one time or another. His life was dominated by the weight of the guilt of his past. Missed opportunities, abuse of his body and the shame had taken its toil. That night, we got down on our knees together and we prayed together in my living room, for peace and healing. I assured him that through Christ, he no longer had to live in fear and with the shame and guilt in his life. Because of what Jesus did at the cross by dying a shameful, sinner's death, all of us were able to live in freedom from that sin and our past. We became redeemed by His blood. When my dad passed away, he received the ultimate healing and the ultimate peace.

Even just a few months before his death, I was on the phone with dad and I asked him a pointed question. I said, "Dad, if you were to die tonight, do you know without a shadow of a doubt where you would spend eternity?" He said, "Yeah buddy, I do, I would be with Jesus." I said, "That's good, because I don't want to spend eternity without you."

To see how our relationship took a complete 180 and how God's grace did such a restorative work in my father's life was nothing short of a miracle. God once again demonstrated that He is the God of redemption and He can turn ashes into a new creation. He can take a man that was broken seemingly beyond repair for many years and through His mercy and grace can make him unbroken without guilt or shame.

It's never too late for God to do that in your life. Don't wait until it's too late to reconcile with the ones you love. Life is too brief to hold grudges and allow the past to blind you to the present. You may be estranged from certain family members, take the first step to allow God to restore that relationship. Maybe it's a marriage that needs to be healed, make the first move today. I am thankful that I had a chance to tell my father that I loved him and that I forgave him.

I love Ephesians 4:31-32, *Let all bitterness and wrath and anger and clamor and slander be put away from you, along with all malice. Be kind to one another, tenderhearted, forgiving one another, as God in Christ forgave you.*

Put away all of your pride, forgive those that need to be forgiven and extend grace to those who need it the most. This requires us to love those who are sometimes frankly unloveable. Who is like that in your life? Who is your Kryptonite? Who is the one person that when you read this full circle story of redemption, that you think about? Trust me, everyone has a Stewart Johnson in their life.

Your Prayers Will Be Answered

You may be searching for answers, you may have prayed for a breakthrough but you are still not seeing results. At times you feel that God is ignoring you or is simply just not doing anything about your pain. In the Old Testament, I am sure Daniel felt the same way. In Daniel chapter 10, we find Daniel crying out to God for an answer to his prayer. After three weeks, God appears to him and this was His response.

"'Relax, Daniel,' he continued, 'don't be afraid. From the moment you decided to humble yourself to receive understanding, your prayer was heard, and I set out to come to you. But I was waylaid by the angel-prince of the kingdom of Persia and was delayed for a good three weeks. But then Michael, one of the chief angel-princes,

intervened to help me. I left him there with the prince of the kingdom of Persia. And now I'm here to help you understand what will eventually happen to your people. The vision has to do with what's ahead.' Daniel 10:12-14 MSG

God explains to Daniel that from the moment Daniel voiced his prayer, He heard him and He began to work on it. Sometimes the answer to our prayer is met with silence because God is at work. The answer requires patience and an attitude that won't quit while you wait. This is great assurance that God isn't sitting back waiting for the last moment to come to the rescue. He never stops fighting for us and He never loses.

He also made it clear to Daniel that sometimes answers are delayed because of the vast spiritual warfare that is going on behind the scenes. Many times we aren't aware of the battle that goes on for our souls, our families, our ministries and especially our relationships. However He promises us that even though we may be persecuted, we are never abandoned. We may get knocked down, but we will not be destroyed because He protects us from the enemy.

If you are like me, you hate waiting on anything. This past week, I waited in the doctor's office for over an hour and a half just to get back to another room where I waited some more. They want you to be on time for your appointment, but why does it even matter? Often life mirrors the doctor's office, hurry up and wait. We spend entire seasons of our life in this perpetual waiting room, just waiting on God to answer our prayers. Maybe that is why Jesus makes it clear that Love is patient. We have to be reminded that God loves us so much that the answers that we sometimes desire isn't necessarily a no, it's just a, not right now.

That answer bothers us in today's culture, because everything is right now. We know what we want and we want it immediately. This instant gratification culture will eventually crash, because we can't always keep up with it. When God answers us in this way, it is sometimes to protect us or simply to let us know that God has something better than we could even imagine or dream for own lives.

When I was a kid, I wasn't a huge fan of puzzles. I am not talking about the toddler puzzles, where you would put a fruit or shape in a space. I am talking about the 10,000 piece puzzles that would take up your entire kitchen table. I would begin the puzzle and when it got hard, I would just give up. I didn't have the patience to see it through until the end.

As an adult I would struggle with the fact that my life was a jigsaw puzzle and I could never see what the end result was and it was a tedious task of putting down one piece at a time, rather than several. There were times I got ahead of God, at least in my mind because I was trying to see the big picture before I was ready.

God doesn't ask us to see the whole puzzle until the end of our lives. He wants us to simply lay down one piece at a time in faith and allow Him to shape the rest of the big picture. To have the patience to lay down one puzzle piece at a time, it takes complete trust that God has the whole picture worked out for our good.

A big part of the waiting game is the lack of trust that we have in Him to provide exactly what we need and the appropriate time we need it. When we really trust Christ with every ounce of our being, then the answer won't really matter because it will be good for us, even if we don't like it or understand it.

Joy in the Pain

What if your prayers aren't answered the way you expect them to be? What if God disrupts your plan with an event that you never expected? Our family learned this difficult lesson when I was ten years old. It was the summer of 1988 and I was perfectly content with being an only child, then things changed. Our whole family went on our annual summer vacation to Panama City Beach, FL, also known as the Redneck Rivera. My mother was sick most of the trip and she didn't know why. She even got car sick on the way down to Florida and on the way back. When we returned from vacation my mom went to the doctor and learned that she was pregnant. At that very moment, I knew that life as an only child would cease to exist. Honestly a big part of me was ready to have a brother or sister. I was intrigued by the possibility. We would even have to move because our duplex that we were living in wasn't big enough for a new baby. That was a good thing for me.

A few weeks later the surprises kept coming. My mom made the announcement that I was going to have two baby sisters. She was expecting twins! I had never seen twins, let alone met twins, so this was shocking to me. This also meant that I would be outnumbered two to one. I am not sure how I felt about that. There was overwhelming joy in our new house and we were so excited about adding to our family. My mom was preparing for two baby girls, which was such a departure from an active ten year old boy. I am sure she was ready to have girls in the house.

In November of 1988, it was a Wednesday night and we were about to leave my grandparents house to go to church, when things took a turn. I was downstairs in the den watching TV and my mom was walking down the stairs to inform me that it was time to go. On her way down the stairs, the heel of her shoe got caught in the carpet and she tumbled down the stairs. I rushed over to her and she said, "Just let me lay here for a second." She then told me to call someone for help and I immediately ran to the phone and called my papaw to come and get us.

We drove to the hospital to get her checked out. We were all fearful that she would lose the babies. The doctors came in and assured us the babies were fine and that she would be ok. It was certainly a scare, but we were all relieved that she and the babies would be fine.

Later that same month, my mom was placed back into Hutcheson Medical Center due to what she thought was a kidney infection, it turns out it was much worse than a simple kidney infection. She was making frequent trips to the bathroom and was cramping uncontrollably and was beginning to get worried. The doctors continued to tell her that she would be ok and the babies were ok. They finally did a scan of the babies and the doctor never came in for the results. He was missing in action. That night her water started leaking and they rushed her into another room and informed her that she was in labor.

At this point of the pregnancy, she was only 26 weeks along. The reality of giving birth to twins prematurely was now upon us. I want to remind you that in those days the medical advances in neonatology didn't exist yet. There wasn't much that could be done to help premature babies and the death rate was very high. We needed a miracle, we needed God to intervene in a way that only He could. We needed Him to show up and provide something that we had never seen in our lives.

At 1:00 am, they would inform my mom and dad that they would have to transport her by ambulance to East Ridge

Hospital, where they had a neonatal unit. Hutcheson wasn't prepared for this type of emergency and she would have to be moved. I am sure that must've been the longest ride in an ambulance ever for my mom and my dad, who rode in the front with the driver. Upon arrival they did another scan, this time the results were read immediately and it wasn't news that they were prepared for. The first baby, Jillian Leigh was stillborn and had been gone for a few days. My mom and dad were devastated. The other twin, Jordan Lynn was receiving all of the nourishment and was very active, Jillian was receiving nothing and she couldn't survive. The stillborn child was causing the labor and she would have to give birth to both babies soon.

Three hours later on December 1, at 4:00am, my mom delivered Jillian first and she was pronounced dead immediately. She weighed just one pound, two ounces. Four minutes later, Jordan Lynn was born and weighed just one pound, nine ounces. She was holding her own, but would have to fight hard to survive. She just wasn't ready to be born and went immediately into the incubator and on a respirator. Her heartbeat was faint and her lungs were severely underdeveloped. My dad was there the whole time comforting my mom. Later he would blame himself and the problems that he struggled with, but it wasn't his fault, it wasn't anyone's fault. It just happened.

On December 6, five days after delivering preemie twins, we would lay one of these precious babies to rest at the cemetery. I can't imagine what mom and dad were feeling, especially knowing that the other twin was in the NICU trying to survive. The precious gift that you have been given by God had to be returned to Him so quickly. We never got to know Jillian Leigh, but she will always be in our hearts. The funeral was very small with just family attending on a Saturday morning.

I remember going to the hospital every single day as my mom went to visit and hold my sister. It was such a roller coaster ride for my parents. One day she would be very active and show signs of improvement. There were other days where it didn't look good at all, days where it didn't look like she was going to make it. She was completely in God's hands. There were people praying for her all across the world and my family felt those prayers.

I would later ask my mom what helped her to get through this time of her life. I knew she would obviously say Jesus. That was evident. She also said me, knowing that she had another child at home. She tried to focus on making sure I had a great Christmas. Sometimes when you go through tragedy, you just need to focus on the needs of others and God finds a way to supply your needs.

That Christmas was as normal as it could've been. On that Christmas morning, we went to the hospital to see Jordan and someone had made Santa hats for all of the babies. It was the smallest hat that I had ever seen. After our visit, we did our normal Christmas and then went back later that night. She was still fighting and we had hope for a Christmas miracle. For the next couple of weeks, we would continue to live at the hospital. I even remember burning popcorn in the break room and stinking up the whole hospital. I will never forget those long visits to East Ridge Hospital. The staff was first class and become attached to Jordan. Everyone was cheering on her fight to stay alive. We believed that God would provide a miracle and that He would breathe life into her lungs for her grow.

On the morning of January 8, the phone rang at our house and told us to come to the hospital. It was a Sunday morning and we were getting ready for church. We never made it to church that day. All of our family showed up at the hospital. The doctor told my parents that they needed to make a decision because there wasn't much time left. Jordan was not showing any signs of improvement and her lungs were just not developing the way we had all hoped. She looked active but her heart rate kept getting slower and slower. They needed to decide whether to leave her on the respirator or take her off. Her little body was exhausted and they knew that they didn't want her to suffer. They made the impossible decision to take her off the respirator and every member of the family was there to say their last goodbyes. That afternoon she came off of the respirator.

The nurse asked if mom would like to hold her and of course she said yes. They ushered her into a small room that had a rocking chair and everyone took turns holding her. The nurse would bring in a stethoscope to check her heartbeat ever so often. She gave one more heroic stand as she held on but her heart couldn't keep up the fight. As my mom was holding her and rocking her, her heart came to a sudden stop and she quietly passed into eternity. I truly believe that Jordan Lynn was transferred directly from my mother's arms into the safe and comforting arms of Jesus. No more pain, no more fight, it was over.

Six weeks after the death of one child, my family had to deal with the death of another baby girl. When we left that hospital, my mom had a tremendous sense of peace like she had never felt before come over her. She was destroyed, but in the midst of the devastation, she had peace to know that they were both together in heaven. They were both God's little angels now and they would suffer no more and were free. That's why my mom made sure the gravestone read, "God's Little Angels."

Our family not only went through one funeral but also a second one in January of 1989. I remember it being a very sad day and it began to snow during the service. Almost as if the peace that passes all understanding was falling on us as pure as the snow. In the midst of the hardest moment, God was there, comforting and weeping with us, just like He did for Lazarus. It was a beautiful moment right in the middle of the pain. I can't imagine losing two children in six weeks, however my mom knew that God wasn't going to leave her or forsake her. Reflecting back almost 26 years later, my mom says that those two babies taught her about patience and love and would strengthen her faith in Christ to a new level.

I am sure there were questions of why and how in my parents mind. Why would God choose to take them from us? How can you move forward after something so tragic? Some of these questions may never be answered. Most of the time it never benefits us to know why, only how we can grow from it and how can God use it for our good. We will be racking our brain forever trying to figure out why, when God wants us to simply trust Him with everything, even loss. Even when life doesn't make sense and our prayers aren't answered the way we expect them to be. We could very easily have shouted out to God to demand answers, but instead we trusted. Even as a ten year old, I saw my mom handle this like a rock and 12 years later when my own daughter was in an NICU fighting to stay alive, I suddenly remembered the strength that was displayed by my mother and the way that she leaned entirely on God to pull her through. God found a way to use even that pain to bring about good.

My mom would go on to help other women after the loss of a child. She didn't waste an experience just because it was a difficult one, she allowed God to use her through the pain to help others. Tremendous blessings can come from tragedies even when we least expect it. God finds a way to pour His blessings on our lives for generations to come even after hope is gone.

My mother wanted to try again to have another child, but she needed to get herself together first and go through the natural grieving process. She knew that she could never replace those two precious angels. God has a unique way of not replacing what you lose, but He finds a way to bless us in new ways beyond our comprehension. Three years later, in January of 1991, my mom lets us know that she was pregnant once again. This time, it was another girl. We were all nervous after what happened the last time. My mom was especially fearful. Every doctor's visit, she would stand in the elevator and pray, "God please let the baby's heart be beating and let her be healthy."

This pregnancy seemed to be as normal as possible and the baby was growing well. On September 6, 1991, Abigail Faith Johnson was born. The Faith part was no accident. Due to the extreme faith that my mom showed, she knew God would provide. Abby was healthy and as perfect as she could be, at least for a little while. That would change when she became my crazy kid sister. She is now almost 23 and is a wonderful wife and mother herself. More than likely if the twins would've survived, there would be no Abby. The generational blessings that God promises to us are so special. If God didn't give us the blessing of Abby, My mother wouldn't have been blessed with her third grandchild, Carson and future grandchildren to come. God's ways are higher and greater than we can ever imagine. When we stress about the way God answers our prayers, we need to learn how to wait on His ultimate blessings to come and they will come and they will be worth it. Sometimes in ways you can never see or think. That's why He is God and we are not.

So even if life throws you a curve ball and your fervent prayers aren't answered the way you expect, we can rest in the assurance that God provides comfort even when your world is ripped apart. Even when the news of tragedy hits, we have a comforter that makes sense of those moments that make no

147

sense to us. He goes to battle for us and hurts when we hurt and cries when we cry. He not only is present during the times of disappointment and loss, He is also the one that helps us rise to the mountaintop again with His restoration power. He restores the broken wings that we suffer and allows us to fly again. He gives us back the joy that is lost when disaster comes and it will come. He even gives the peace after the chaos ensues.

My mom is living proof that you can find peace and happiness after tragedy. Life can move forward even after you think your world has been destroyed, such a beautiful picture of God's unending grace. That is the kind of God that loves us and died for us. That is the kind of grace and mercy He provides to all of His children. He will find a way in the wilderness, even when there seems to be no way out!

CHAPTER 13
THE COMEBACK

On January 8, 2000, my favorite NFL team, the Tennessee Titans, were playing at home in the first round of the playoffs against the Buffalo Bills. This was the Titan's first foray into the playoffs since they moved to Tennessee. This was the kind of game that you will always remember where you were watching it. I was at my Pappaw's service station, watching on a little TV with my Uncle Rick.

The Bills kicked a field goal with 16 seconds left to take a 16-15 lead. The game was over, at least everyone thought. There was very little time on the clock and the Bills were kicking off to the Titans. There wasn't enough time for a good return and then one last pass into the end zone, so we knew the kick return would be it for the Titans. Bills kicker, Steve Christie kicked it short to the up man, Lorenzo Neal. I knew immediately that he couldn't take it back, he was too slow, but then he handed it off to Frank Wycheck, which happened to be my favorite Titan. Wycheck threw the ball across the field and it was caught by Kevin Dyson. Dyson ran down the sideline untouched for 75 yards for the game winning score. This play would forever be tabbed, the Music City Miracle.

Let's face it, I thought the Titans were dead in the water but I am really glad I didn't turn off the TV. I would have missed the greatest last second comeback in the history of the NFL. That would have been completely devastating. It proved once again that comebacks are possible and attainable if we don't give up. As long as there is still time on the clock, there is always hope.

We live in a culture, where everyone loves a comeback, whether it's your favorite football team or favorite band or actor. We always want to believe that even the impossible can be transformed into the possible. Deep down inside, we all have the potential for a comeback, whether it's a comeback in your walk with Christ, your marriage, career, financial situation or even your ministry.

Everyone loves a comeback, especially Jesus because He is cheering for us much more than anyone ever will in our life. We serve a God that orchestrated the biggest comeback in the history of mankind. Jesus died. Everyone had lost hope witnessing His brutal death. However three days later, He made His comeback being raised from the dead and proclaiming victory over death. Don't you think if the God of redemption can orchestrate that type of victory, He can also orchestrate your comeback as well?

Today is your moment to believe that there is hope for you, despite the trial that you are facing. You may be far from God or you may have just drifted away, He is still with you and hasn't left you. Things may look very bleak in your life, you may feel like your whole world is hopeless, but God has that unique ability to recover what you have lost and restore the hope in you.

It begins with you trusting that God can bring you back to Him and believing that He can heal the wounds in your heart that you have experienced, even if they were self-inflicted. You may feel like you are running out of time, like the Titans were and you have exhausted all of your resources. Things look simply impossible, just remember, that is the moment God stages His greatest comebacks.

There is a recovery story in the Old Testament that involved a man named Elisha.

One day the guild of prophets came to Elisha and said, "You can see that this place where we're living under your leadership is getting cramped—we have no elbow room. Give us permission to go down to the Jordan where each of us will get a log. We'll build a roomier place." Elisha said,"Go ahead." One of them then said, "Please! Come along with us!" He said, "Certainly." He went with them. They came to the Jordan and started chopping down trees. As one of them was felling a timber, his axehead flew off and sank in the river. "Oh no, master!" he cried out. "And it was borrowed!" The Holy Man said, "Where did it sink?" The man showed him the place. He cut off a branch and tossed it at the spot. The axehead floated up. "Grab it," he said. The man reached out and took it. 2 Kings 6:1-7

The axe head that was lost was very valuable and the man that lost it didn't even own it. Many of us have lost things in our lives that were extremely valuable. I am not talking about expensive sunglasses, although I have lost several of those. I am talking about the things that matter the most to us. The things that you never wanted to lose but it happened and now you are left in the ashes. I am talking about the very things that you are willing to die for.

The good news is that God always finds a way to show us exactly where we lost it and always points us in the right direction. He will guide us where we need to be, but He also expects us to reach out and get it because sometimes we have to fight to get back what we lost. You have to ask yourself, are you willing to fight for the important things in life, including your relationship with Christ, the most important relationship in your life? Everything in our lives, flows from that relationship, including other relationships.

You may be where I was, hanging by the final thread of hope. Some of you may feel like your endurance is running out and you're tired of waiting. You may read passages like 1 Corinthians 10:13, *No test or temptation that comes your way is beyond the course of what others have had to face. All you need to remember is that God will never let you down; he'll never let you be pushed past your limit; he'll always be there to help you come through it."*

After reading that, you may think to yourself, how can that be true or maybe, just maybe God has overestimated my capacity for trials and pain. I understand where you may be and I want you to know that the hope of Christ rises to the occasion every single time.

You may be exhausted but your breakthrough is on its way. Don't stop at the one yard line just before the breakthrough. Sometimes we quit right before our miracle. I want to encourage you not to do that, keep moving forward and believe.

If your marriage has been filled with disappointments, it doesn't have to stay that way, things can change but you will never experience the joy of a holy marriage if you quit on the one yard line just before the touchdown.

You may have prodigals in your life. It may be a son, daughter, spouse, mother or father that you are praying for. They are counting on you. You have been praying for them for many years and things just aren't improving. The easy thing would be to quit, but I want to encourage you to press on and keep fighting.

My mother prayed for her prodigal, my dad, for over 30 years and you read the rest of the story. The prayers and persistence paid off. As long as you are still breathing, there is always hope!

God Can Still Use You

For God's gifts and His call are irrevocable. —**Romans 11:29**

God has given each of us gifts to be used for the work of the Kingdom. Just because you have failed in some area, doesn't mean you are a failure. God can use the sin that you have committed to change you and use your experiences in the ministry that He has called you to. He always takes what was meant for evil and transforms it to good.

God's word says these gifts are irrevocable. They can't be taken away. As God transforms your heart from death to life, He can also transform your mess into your message. He can use your test to shape your testimony. The scars of your past can no longer be used against you. God does a miraculous thing with those battle wounds. He uses them to teach others. All of a sudden the stark reminders of your pain are now being used to remind others that God's grace is miraculous and sufficient for all of us, no matter your story. Your battle wounds may save someone else from obtaining the same wounds.

Through my own situation, I've had the opportunity to pour into other people who are dealing with the same issues. I have been provided a collection of experiences that were meant to destroy my life, now are being used as weapons against the enemy.

I heard Wayne Cordeiro say that *"The best vegetables come from sifted soil, which proves that God grows the best stuff from sifted soil. Sifting ratifies us to teach. You teach out of scars, not just out of theory and theology."*

Look at the people in the Bible that God used in amazing ways, who first had to walk through seasons of struggle.

Whether it was Peter who had anger issues or Paul who was a murderer, both of these men are prime examples of great comeback stories.

Peter was the special guest speaker on Pentecost and thousands decided to follow Christ that day and that began the history of the Christian Church. Paul would go from persecuting Christians to be the greatest single influence on the spread of the Gospel since the beginning of time. God proved once again that who you were, doesn't have to be who you are and it certainly doesn't have to define where you are going.

Not only did God restore their hearts to Him, He increased their platforms to shine the light of Christ to the world. He can do the same in your life, your platform for whatever you are wired to do, can increase through the grace of God and your faithfulness to Him. He can open up doors to reach people that you would never have before.

In my own life, I have experienced the same grace that Peter and Paul received and the good news is, you can to. These are some of the ways God is changing my heart daily and He can change yours as well.

I was.... A self reliant man, Thought I had it all figured out.

I am becoming…. a man that relies completely on Christ with a heart of surrender.

I was…. An angry person, filled with anxiety.

I am becoming…. A man filled with the spirit, and a calm assurance of Christ.

I was.... A liar.

I am becoming.... A man of integrity, filled with the truth of God's word.

I was.... A man who used words to defend.

I am becoming.... A man who uses words to breathe life into those I come in contact with.

I was.... A man who used the word of God just for sermon prep.

I am becoming.... Someone who hungers for more of God's word every day.

I was.... A hurricane, destructive in many ways.

I am becoming.... A gentle man that is concerned for others more than myself

I was.... Arrogant, filled with deceit

I am becoming.... Broken by God and raised in Humility

I was.... Selfish

I am becoming.... More like Him and less like me

I was.... A man who struggled with control issues

I am becoming.... A man who understands that control belongs to God, I can rest in knowing He's in control.

I was.... A man that felt God was running away from Him after my wife left.

I am becoming.... A man that knows that God never left my side and that He was always drawing me to Him.

I was.... Hopeless

I am becoming…. Hopeful because my hope is found in Jesus alone. That's it. He's all I need!

I was…. A man that prayed but it was casual.

I am becoming…. A man that fervently prays with intention. A man facedown before God!

I was…. Filled with Pride, I didn't need help.

I am becoming…. Humbled by Him, recognizing when I am weak, He is at His strongest.

I was…. Floating through life with no accountability

I am becoming…. A man with utmost accountability and safeguards in place. A prayer support system that's incredible.

I was…. Hidden in the shadows, kept everything in.

I am becoming…. Transparent, full disclosure.

I was…. A man That took everything for granted, especially my family.

I am becoming…. Thankful for everything that God has blessed me with!

I was…. A man with inner turmoil that I couldn't explain.

I am becoming…. A man filled with Joy even in the midst of my circumstances!

Don't Forget the Containers

God doesn't just desire that you get just a taste of His many blessings. **Ephesians 3:20 says,** *Now all glory to God, who is able, through his mighty power at work within us, to accomplish infinitely more than we might ask or think.* He is able to accomplish infinitely more than we can ever imagine or hope for. Which means, whatever your expectations of God were before, eliminate them because they are extremely low. Our God is going to barrel you over with His blessings!

I absolutely love the passage in Romans 5 that says, *There's more to come: We continue to shout our praise even when we're hemmed in with troubles, because we know how troubles can develop passionate patience in us, and how that patience in turn forges the tempered steel of virtue, keeping us alert for whatever God will do next. In alert expectancy such as this, we're never left feeling shortchanged. Quite the contrary—we can't round up enough containers to hold everything God generously pours into our lives through the Holy Spirit! Romans 5:3-5*

That is one of those scriptures that you put on your dashboard. You need to frame it and put it on your wall. The writer of this book, Paul, is saying, don't get caught up in the now, keep pushing and clawing and scratching. Remain steadfast because it will transform into a rock solid virtue. Stay alert because God is about to do a new thing.

It doesn't say pay attention to what's in the past or even what your current situation looks like. It says patience keeps us alert to what God is doing next. In due time, God will pour and continue to pour His blessings into you and through you. It will be like a boat that doesn't have a plug in it. The water will be rushing in faster than you can scoop it out. You won't be able to find a big enough bucket to hold it all.

I don't know about you, but that's good news to me. Brace yourself because the blessings will come, the opportunities will come, God will open up the doors that you thought would never be opened and close the ones that should be slammed shut. So when you are tired or when you are walking through a tough season, whatever you do, don't forget the containers that God is about to pour into your life.

The Church's Role in the Comeback

"Maybe if you have money, health and a busy schedule, you don't feel the need to fellowship with other Christians. But when the storms of life hit — and they will — suddenly you'll find nobody's there. If you remain shallow in your relationship to your local church, you will lose out on the support of other Christians when you need it most." — Luis Palau

After my crash and when everything fell apart, I could have very easily turned my back on the church. I could have walked out and never returned like many of my friends who have been broken. As long as we are human, brokenness is inevitable. It is where we choose to land is what is important.

Will we turn our back on the church and our community of faith or will be embrace the church as a safe haven for the weary and a house of restoration? I didn't let this shake my faith and the confidence that I have in the bride of Christ. Many people however choose another way in the opposite direction for a variety of reasons. One of which may be the fact that they were hurt by the "church". When people say I have been hurt by the church, what do they really mean?

The institution of the church itself is not damaging the name of Jesus. They are not the one causing harm. What they really mean is that a person or group of people they associate with the Church has wounded them. As is often the case, thinking or speaking of their hurt in such personal terms stirs up painful emotions.

It is hard to talk about our wounds and say the names of our friends, pastors or mentors who have caused the pain. Sometimes it feels like death to say exactly what they have done to us. Each time we retell the story, something inside us replays our experience that, in one way or another, told us that we were not needed or wanted. However, if we are ever to move past this kind of hurt and journey toward restoration that is exactly what we must do. Forgiveness can only exist where the truth is present and spoken.

The problem is we usually don't make it that far. Instead of biblically working out our differences, we run. We decide that this whole church thing isn't worth it. We hear people make statements like, "I am a Christian but I don't need the church." I get it, I understand it, but I don't agree with it. We all need the church because we were designed to live and grow in our faith in a community of believers. When we hit rock bottom, we especially need others who are going pick us up off the floor when we fall and believe me, we will fall.

If you have been hurt by the "church," I want to apologize on behalf of the church. I had nothing to do with your situation, but I understand your pain. The sad thing is I can't promise it won't happen again because the very people that make up a church are just merely imperfect humans filled with as many issues as you have. As long as there are imperfect people in this world, there will always be imperfect churches. Let me save you time and energy, if you are looking for the perfect church, it will take until you die, because it doesn't exist.

Instead of looking for the imperfections in the church, discover the benefits of allowing the body of Christ to lift you back to where you need to be. The church's role of restoring should be simple. I see a church that restores the wandering and broken not to the place where you were but to a whole new level that you couldn't have imagined for yourself. I see a church that guides you to the next step in your journey with gentle hands. I see a church that extends grace to those who don't feel worthy to accept it. I see a church that believes in you, no matter where you have been and what you have done or even how long your list of sins may be. I see a church that accepts you with your flaws and everything that entails. I see a church that challenges but never condemns through the word of God. I see a church that will reach out their hands and be willing to walk the extra mile with you just like the good Samaritan did. I see a church that will equip you, empower you and release you into service to others. I see a church that is built on the foundation of grace and forgiveness.

The church today has become so focused on being a, "come as you are church." We believe in grace, but they have to come to us first. Almost as if we are standing on a tired principle. A "come as you are church" indicates that you are waiting for them to show up. We need to be a "go where they are church" where they are waiting on us to show up! There are countless people living in homes all around us that need to know that there is healing and hope available. We need to meet people where they are, around the dinner table, sitting in a living room, out in the yard or even at the grocery store. That is where life is happening and they are waiting on the church to come to them. You are the church, you are the vessel that can carry the hope of Christ into your neighborhood and your city. While it's great to create a welcoming environment in your church, let's not forget the real opportunity to be the church is found outside the actual church building.

That is the church I envision. That is the people that all of us can become. Ask yourself the question, is that what my church looks like? If you are hurting, or if you are currently trying to rise from the ashes, find a church that will open up their arms to you and love you unconditionally. This is the only way you can fully heal.

Allow this community to help with the healing process and allow God to use them to give you the support that you will need during this season. Then in turn, one day you will be the one who will be the support system for someone just like you. If you are walking through a Saturday season, find a healthy, vibrant church, one that is full of life and dive in!

It's Not Over

God knows exactly what we need and at precisely the right time we need it. One day I was feeling extremely low and someone texted me a song by Israel Houghton. I love Israel's music but on this day, I didn't feel like listening to anything that had to do with hope. Things looked really hopeless in my life.

I reluctantly pushed play and about 30 seconds into the song, my eyes were filled with tears and began to cry out to God. After the first couple of times through the song, I began to sing along. I truly believed the words that I was listening to.

These were the words I began to sing and these are the words I encourage you with today that no matter what it feels like or looks like, it's simply not over. Don't underestimate God's perfect timing in your situation. The moment you think it's over is the moment that God gives you pleasant surprises.

Its Not Over, Its Not Finished
Its Not Ending, Its Only The Beginning
When God Is In It, All Things Are New

I Know It's Darkest Just Before Dawn
Might Be The Hardest Season You Experience
I Know It Hurts, Wont Be Too Long
You're Closer Than You Think You Are
You're Closer Than You've Been Before

Look To The Sky, Help Is On The Way
Its Not Over, Its Not Finished
Its Not Ending, Its Only The Beginning
When God Is In It All Things Are New

Something Is Moving, Turning Around
Seasons Are Changing, Everything Is Different Now
Here Comes The Sun, Piercing The Clouds
You're Closer Than You Think You Are
You're Closer Than You've Been Before

Its Not Over, Its Not Finished
Its Not Ending, Its Only The Beginning
When God Is In It, All Things Are New

A few years ago, I had a friend that went to see the first Lord of the Rings movie in the theater. He wasn't schooled on the finer ins and outs of all things Lord of the Rings. I will admit without shame that I am not either. Unbeknownst to him, he didn't realize that this movie was only part one of the trilogy. He left disappointed and felt cheated that the story didn't end, but was to be continued.

Some of you may be reading this book and you are waiting for the epic Hollywood ending, where the guy gets the girl and lives happily ever after. We all want to get to the positive, wonderful conclusion. The only problem is, this isn't the end of the story, it continues on. This chapter is completed, but a new chapter begins. My story is no different than yours, in the fact that it continues on. The fact is God didn't heal my marriage, but He healed my heart and gave me the opportunity to live life again.

Earlier in the book, I shared a story about David and the transformation that God did in his heart. That change didn't come without pain, suffering and loss, however when it was time to move forward, God gave him peace and clarity to move on with his life with a renewed passion and a laser focused vision.

In the story I made mention that David and Bathsheba's son would live only a few days. What I didn't tell you is what happened between the child's birth and tragic death. David was faced with a seemingly impossible situation. His son was fighting for his life and the outcome looked very bleak. The scripture says that David inquired of God for the child; and David fasted and went and lay all night on the ground. He committed completely to the healing of his child. The elders of his household stood beside him in order to raise him up from the ground, but he was unwilling and would not eat food with them. He was so invested in the healing of the child that he poured all of himself out to God with hopes of a bright outcome. In the end, it wasn't to be.

After seven days of pleading with God and fasting, the child finally succumbed to illness. The Bible says the elders were so afraid to break the news to David they were fearful of his reaction to this devastating loss. They weren't sure if he would harm himself or others. David knew what had happened, he saw the faces of the elders and saw them whispering. David quickly said, "Is the child dead?" They confirmed the news and what David did next was completely a God moment and a testimony to God's grace.

2 Samuel 12:20- *So David arose from the ground, washed, anointed himself, and changed his clothes; and he came into the house of the LORD and worshiped. Then he came to his own house, and when he requested, they set food before him and he ate.*

David's response left the elders of the house baffled. They questioned David's reaction and more than likely questioned his sanity.

21 David's servants said to him, "Why are you doing this? When the baby was still alive, you fasted and you cried. Now that the baby is dead, you get up and eat food."

22 David said, "While the baby was still alive, I fasted, and I cried. I thought, 'Who knows? Maybe the Lord will feel sorry for me and let the baby live.' 23 But now that the baby is dead, why should I fast? I can't bring him back to life. Someday I will go to him, but he cannot come back to me."

When the child was alive, David gave it all to God and rightfully left the situation completely in His hands. When the child died, he instinctively knew that he was gone. But why would David react so quickly to the death of his child? His reaction seemed so cold and emotionless. The answer is simple, because he was so connected to God that he had complete affirmation and peace from the Father. David wholeheartedly accepted God's final answer to his prayer to God on behalf of the child.

David did every single thing he could, but in the end it wasn't meant to be. God gave a clear, final determination and the answer was unfortunately, "No." Many times, there is a certain peace that falls over us when we know in our heart that we did everything possible in our situation. This makes it possible for us to stand up from our prayer position, clean our face, worship God and finally start eating again. I didn't say it wasn't difficult, but God's peace gives us the freedom to experience life after the storm and to move forward with the next chapter of life with boldness.

David knew that this chapter of life was over but he also knew that the next chapter had unending possibilities. Throughout death, defeat and prayers being answered in ways that we don't expect, God is still God and God is still good. Moving forward boldly with Christ doesn't mean you are being insensitive to the past or the present, it just means that you have confidence in the promises of God for a bright future.

Moving forward is a natural progression that we all must go through, no matter how difficult it may be to do so. We must discern the voice of God to hear His answers with clarity. Many times, we are waiting on an answer from God after He has already given it. We either miss it or we ignore it, because it's not the answer we are looking for! I have been known to do this in my own life. God has revealed something to me and I send it back to Him with a counter offer. He doesn't work that way, His word is final. We must accept God's decisions and move forward.

What tends to happen is we will allow God's "no" to paralyze us. We will waste years worrying about something that God has forgotten about long ago. He wants us to realize that "no" doesn't mean stop living, it actually means begin to live again with new mercies, new dreams, new hope, new relationships and a new view of His plan for your life. Don't be frozen in time by your disappointments, thaw out and move on.

I had to learn in my own life to accept God's answers to the difficult questions. Once I chose to listen and accept this determination, a tremendous amount of peace came over me.

I got up from my prayer position and made the intentional decision to accept it and move forward with my life. Once I made that decision, God began to bless my life in new ways. Ways that I never thought were possible. I stopped looking in the rearview mirror and I began to focus entirely on the future that God has planned for me. I believe my greatest days are ahead and the new adventure is just beginning.

This may be the last page of the book, but it isn't the final page of my story or yours. Your story isn't over. Imagine if Peter's story ended after he denied Christ three times or if Paul's story ended before his miraculous conversion from the evil Saul. What if Joshua's story would have ended after walking around the walls of Jericho only 5 times or if Nehemiah's story would've ended before he lifted one finger to rebuild the wall? You may be living in the darkest chapter of your life, but that is not the way the story ends. God has mapped out what the future looks like and we each have so much story to live and so much more love to give. If you don't like how your story is playing out, chase after the will of God with vigor and do something about it, don't wait. Today begins the next chapter of your journey, this is your chance to dust off the ashes that you have been consumed with and RISE! Rejoice, because God has made you Unbroken!

ACKNOWLEDGEMENTS

First and foremost, I would like to thank the two most amazing kids in the entire universe. Jada and Skyler. You are daddy's heartbeat and I love you very much. I am blessed with an amazing family. The journey I have been on over the last couple of years has changed our family. We have seen a revival take place and we have grown closer to each other and closer to Jesus.

Mom, you are a testimony of grace and mercy. Thanks for always being there for me and showing me what Jesus looks like. My sister Abby, my brother in-law Jon and my amazing nephew, Carson. I love each of you, thanks for your undying support of me. Keivin and Melody, Rick and Tonya, Christina and Chad, Jonathan, Mimi and Papaw, Grandma and Frank. Thanks for being such a special family. Justin, thanks for being a brother to me and for the late night texts that have kept me going through tough times.

I have so many friends and mentors that have been so supportive over the years. Dr. Mark and Jan Gregory, thanks for being wonderful mentors for me and ushering me through my first publishing adventure. Thanks to Jacob and Rhea for your many prayers and accountability. Tim and Vicki Gates, thanks for your mentorship and being like parents to me. I would like to thank my other sources of prayer support and accountability, Rick Legg, Jonathan Trees and Michael Chaney. Thanks Michael for asking me the tough questions. Chris and Emily Hughes and all of the folks at Life Church in Franklin, NC, thanks for your friendship and believing in me.

Ron Cook and the people at the Care for Pastors organization, thank you for what you do for pastors that are broken all across the country. I believe in your ministry and your calling to heal the hurting. Nick and Christy Queitsch, thank you for believing in me and my ministry. I would have never planted a church if it wasn't for you. Shane Harden, Greg Pullen, Rick Cone, Gary Baldus, Brett Rickey, Kevin Wallace, Travis Jones, David and Karen Quiroz, Marcus and Kim Wright, thank you for always supporting me and your encouragement.

I had the most amazingly talented creatives working on this project. Mike Hall and Melinda Horsey, you are both geniuses, thanks for your fellowship and creating with me. Blake Morgan, you did an amazing job on the cover. You are a great friend. Heather Ebert, you are an editing ninja. Thanks for helping me shape this book. Adam York, thanks for your friendship and encouragement.

Stephanie Morris, thank you for adding your editing prowess to this project. Thank you for your friendship and support.

Leah, thanks for your friendship and your motivation. This book would have never been finished without you stretching me and challenging me. You will never know what a blessing you were to me through this process.

ABOUT THE AUTHOR

Jeremy Johnson's passion became evident at the early age of two when he stood behind a ceramic owl statue and pretended to preach in his relatives' living room. At nine, he accepted Christ as his personal Savior and by 17 sought out opportunities to lead worship and speak in various services throughout the southeast, where he was raised. To this day, his creativity encourages people who are far from the truth to learn about and know God's grace is sufficient for them. He develops leaders by inspiring them to pursue their callings and has a deep desire to see and be involved with successful church planting.

His personal ministry started in 2000 when he served as pastor of students and college ministries – seeing a growth in weekly attendance from 12 to 75 students. In 2001, he established his own evangelical organization, J2 Ministries traveling throughout the country impacting thousands for Christ. 2007 was the year God directed Jeremy Johnson to invest in community and build relationships starting as an Associate Pastor at the local church level and then as Founder and Lead Pastor for a new church plant in Orlando, Florida. Similar to the preaching he did at two, Element church's humble beginnings were in a living room, but grew from six dedicated believers to a congregation of 140 regular worshipers in the span of a year.

Father of two beautiful children, Jada and Skyler. Jeremy's world was turned upside down when his wife of 13 years left him in late 2012 and four months later filed for divorce. Though there was no moral failure involved, Jeremy was confronted with the reality of his focus and readily harnessed the blame for his failed marriage. Through God's miraculous grace and mercy the months following became a time of incredible spiritual growth. Jeremy garnered the support of a new community including two counsellors proficient in the process of healing pastors, a team of 80+ prayer warriors and six men who are his personal board of Directors that have kept him accountable and encouraged.

Jeremy's book, "Unbroken"- Discovering Wholeness through the Shattered Pieces of Life", which is based on his journey of restoration, is his first book. His passion to be the leader God has created him to be continues through the healing of scars and the connecting with those who are far from God on a deep level. The scripture that has been his anchor of hope is Galatians 6:9. *Let us not grow weary of doing good, for in due time the harvest will come – if we refuse to give up.*

CONNECT WITH JEREMY

EMAIL- J2MINISTRIES@GMAIL.COM

SOCIAL MEDIA

FACEBOOK- @JEREMYJOHNSONMINISTRIES
@UNBROKENBOOK

TWITTER- @JEREMYJOHNSON1
@UNBROKENTHEBOOK

INSTAGRAM- @JEREMYJOHNSON1

Don't Give Up!
Gal. 6:9

Made in the USA
Charleston, SC
05 September 2014